Best wishes

Down the Line

The Julian Broddle Story

By

© Julian Broddle 2017

Published by Babysteps Publishing Limited
http://babystepspublishinglimited.com

Contact: Kevin A Long

ISBN-13:978-1975916503

ISBN-10:1975916506

Disclaimer

Although the author and publisher have made every effort to ensure that the information in this book was correct at press time, the author and publisher do not assume and hereby disclaim any liability to any party for any loss, damage, or disruption caused by errors or omissions, whether such errors or omissions result from negligence, accident, or any other cause.

Table of Contents

Dedication

This book is dedicated to my three children, who are now young adults. My biggest regret in life is that in 1998 when your Mum and I split up, that I wasn't there for you and became the distant Dad who rarely saw his children. I know I cannot make that up to you but I hope that by reading the honest story about my life that you will understand me a little better and, maybe one day, forgive me and accept me. Life is too short to leave things left unsaid, so hopefully by reading this book you feel a little closer to me and understand the love I have for all three of you.

Acknowledgement

I am writing this credit to a man I have only known for a few years but without him, I doubt I would have ever finished this book. Steven Lawther is a Raith Rovers diehard, and can be seen at most games with his wife and daughter Grace. I got to know Steven when he asked me for an interview for his book he was writing about Raith Rovers. The book, Unthinkable, is a fantastic read about the period of the clubs' history when we went on to win the Coca Cola League Cup in 1994, against the mighty Celtic.

It is a brilliant read, not just for Rovers fans, but for anybody who loves sport, and especially the underdog. It tells the story of Raith taking on one of the biggest supported clubs in Britain and its incredible history, and after extra time and penalties, overcoming the odds to win and go on to represent Scotland in Europe in 1995. I gave my interview to Steven and just by talking to him; I could feel his enthusiasm for the club and the book he was writing.

When the book was published and I got a copy and I couldn't put it down. The book brought back some amazing memories for me, and I couldn't stop smiling throughout, and I thank him for making an old man very happy.

I started writing my own book about three years plus ago, and originally, was meant just for my three children as a memoir. I got in touch with Steven to seek some advice, and he gave me the inspiration to have a go at writing a book that could be published and ready by fans of the clubs I had played for. I wrote when I got the chance, but as I was in the Police at the time, it was very difficult to write when on rest days as I needed that time to recover from the stresses of work. The final straw was when I was arrested and dismissed by South Yorkshire Police. This killed my writing enthusiasm and it was a dark period of my life. My thoughts were elsewhere and I could not even switch my laptop on.

After a while, I decided to get back in touch with Steven and once again, he gave me the inspiration to get by backside in gear and finish it off. He was even prepared to come down to Yorkshire and interview me on chapters I had already written and give me advice on what I still needed to write. He helped me pull it all together and turn it into the book you have in your hand now, even helping me find a publisher. Without him, I wouldn't have got my story onto the book aisles. I thank you again my friend. I will never forget what you did for me and I don't think I will ever be able to repay you.

Foreword

When Julian contacted to ask if I would write this foreword for his book, I was honoured and felt very proud. I like to think I helped Julian in his career by giving him a chance to get regular football at Scunthorpe United, and then in the second tier at a higher standard when I bought him for Barnsley.

The fact that I signed Julian twice in my managerial career shows how much I rated him as a footballer and a person. He never let me down on or off the pitch. In 134 appearances for Scunthorpe United, he scored 32 goals which for a utility player was a wonderful achievement and proved my judgement right in signing him and placing my faith in him. When I left Scunthorpe United and moved to Barnsley Football Club it made sense to make Julian one of my signings, and again he proved me right.

Julian was a very skilful footballer. He once told me that one of his later managers wanted Julian to play left back and get the ball from the keeper then launch it as long as possible for the strikers to chase. I knew Julian well enough, and coached him long enough, to know that this was a terrible waste of his ability. He had one of the best left foots in the game at the time and that he also possessed tremendous pace and ability. Julian needed to be encouraged to go forward, and pass the ball and get crosses into the box. That was how he would cause the opposition problems.

The only problem in my whole time working with Julian that I ever had with him was his haircut, or more accurately, his lack of a haircut. I remember telling Julian and two other Barnsley lads to get down to the barbers and sort out their hair. They must have misunderstood me as all three of them only had a trim!

When I was at Lincoln, Julian once came and trained with us. He knew a few of the lads from his Sheffield United days, so he settled in very quickly and it was great having him there with the team. I would have loved to have signed him a third time, but we didn't have the finances to do a deal so he returned to Scotland and continued on his career. I always kept an eye out for Julian when possible, and with the right club and manager, I know he could have gone on and played at the highest level. I am delighted that he found success towards the end of his career with Raith Rovers.

When Julian and his partner, Jane, got in touch in 2017, and said they were coming over to Scunthorpe to be a special guest at a match against Sheffield United, I was delighted to see them at my home. It was wonderful talking about football stories from Scunthorpe United and Barnsley. Julian said he could have sat with Margaret and me all day, and I felt the same.

When I was first told and then read about the drug accusation about Julian, my reaction was one of shock and disbelief. I knew the boy and man very well and I knew that this just couldn't be true. I did not hesitate to offer him my support when we eventually spoke. The incident with South Yorkshire Police could have ruined lesser men. But I know Julian Broddle and his strength of character and I know he will come out of the situation a better and stronger person. I am proud to know him and consider him a friend. In both his professional and private life he showed incredible loyalty and never let me down. I will always be there for him.

Allan Clarke

Me and Allan

Introduction

Mondays aren't usually the best day for most people but the start to this particular week has turned out to be better than most for me.

As I write it has been just four months since I was dismissed from South Yorkshire Police, and although I have tried to get on with my life as best I can, being sacked from a job that you love is a tremendous blow and not something that you can just get over quickly. Aside from having to deal with the lurid tabloid headlines branding me a 'dodgy cop', I have lost the togetherness that comes from being in the Police service.

I still have many good friends in South Yorkshire Police and I still get invited on nights out by my ex-colleagues but, much like being part of a football club, I miss the day-to-day camaraderie, fun and team spirit. I can't escape the fact that I am no longer a cop whilst my friends are.

Yet the hardest part of my recent experience has been explaining to people in my life what happened and my side of the story. This morning I sat down to do exactly that with one of my former managers Allan Clarke. The two most influential people in my football life were Jimmy Nicholl and Allan Clarke. Jimmy Nicholl was a fantastic motivator in the later stages of my career at Raith Rovers, but it was Allan Clarke who had the greatest influence on my early career as a young footballer.

Allan played for the brilliant Leeds United team of the Don Revie era and would go on to become an established England international. He was my manager at Scunthorpe and Barnsley at the start of my career and would later become a friend, someone who I respected and trusted. Allan was his own man and told you it as it was. His forthrightness, honesty and belief in his own ability was sometimes mistaken for arrogance, I knew him well enough to know that was just Allan Clarke. He wanted the best for his players and staff and if it was good enough for the great Leeds United team, then it was good enough for Scunthorpe United or Barnsley. He stood by his words and actions.

I had caught up with Allan and his wife Margaret at the start of this season, when I was a guest at Scunthorpe United against Sheffield United. It was a privilege to spend time in their company and will always be something that I will treasure. At the time, I was aware of my situation with work but as I was so embarrassed about it, I never mentioned it. Perhaps I thought at the time that if I didn't talk about it or think about it, it would go away. But it hadn't and now that I had been dismissed I knew I had to talk to my old manager.

I had thought about emailing him many times over the months, but couldn't face it as I was ashamed knowing that he would have read the press reports. I was saddened that he might have believed them and think that I had let him down. But I knew that out of respect for him, I had to let him know what had happened. As someone who was hugely influential in my career, I also wanted to let him know that I was writing this book and to ask his permission to talk about the influence he had on my career and, if possible, ask him to write a little about his view of me as a player.

I sat down at my dining table with my laptop, and started to write a long email to Allan and Margaret Clarke. I explained what had happened and why I felt I had to let them know my side of the story. I apologised for not letting them know sooner and asked for their forgiveness. I knew that Alan still did media work and is closely associated with Leeds United, so I said that I would understand if they didn't want to be associated with me, in order to protect his own reputation. I finished what I needed to say and pressed the send button.

I told my partner Jane that I had finally sent the message that I had avoided for so long. I told her that they will probably read it and if I was lucky, he might reply with a polite message saying 'thanks, but no thanks'. Jane replied that at least it was now done and to wait and see.

A few minutes later we were in the garage clearing some old boxes and my mobile rang. I grabbed it and started to walk to the back of the garden to get a better reception. It was a man's voice on the line, and it started with "Julian, it is Allan."

At first, I thought "Alan?" Then it clicked, it was the boss, Allan Clarke. Just twenty minutes after pressing send on the email, here he was calling me. I thanked him for calling me so quickly and he told me that his wife Margaret had said not to call me so quickly, as she felt it must have been difficult for me to write that email. But he said he couldn't wait as he has seen the media headlines and that his only reaction was that he didn't believe any of it as he knew that 'Julian Broddle would never take drugs.'

Can you imagine how I felt after hearing those words from a man who I looked up to and who I considered a living legend? I was smiling like a Cheshire cat. We went on to chat for ages and he told me that he was happy for me to write about my times with him as my manager and friend and would be proud to provide a foreword for the book. I felt incredibly happy and emotional at his friendship and support.

To think that less than an hour before I was wondering whether he would ever talk to me again! We said our goodbyes and as the phone call ended I felt like I had just won the lottery. Allan Clarke has an amazing history and is friends with many greats from the world of football, yet here he was taking the time out of his day to call me straight away to reassure me and give me the words I needed to hear. That he knew that I would never knowingly jeopardise my career by taking drugs. It was what I knew to be true, but something that I doubted that others would accept. What a man and what a friend.

A few minutes later, I received a message from Steven Lawther, who had been helping me pull the book together, saying that we finally had a name for the book and that the publisher would be in touch to finalise the details of publication. What a Monday, a day that has turned out to be a brilliant day for me and hopefully a turning point after a challenging and difficult time. As one of my favourite quotes states, "Though no one can go back and make a brand-new start, anyone can start from new and make a brand-new beginning."

The title of this book, 'Down the Line' was suggested by a work contact of Stevens called Peter Boydell, who very appropriately is a big Barnsley fan. I'd like to thank him for it as it is a title that means a lot to me. Having spent my career on the left wing or left side, it is a phrase I heard a lot from team-mates, managers and supporters over the years.

It also refers to the fact I am now sitting here, many years later, reflecting on my life. I have had many great times at the football clubs I have had the privilege to represent and my career in the Police Force has also brought me many happy memories. Yet, like in most people's lives there have also been challenges and difficult times. This book is the honest story of my life, the highs and the lows.

I know that many people will always choose to believe the newspaper headlines about recent events. That is their right, but everything I have written is the truth and I hope that anyone who takes the time to read my story will understand that. I hope you enjoy my story.

Julian Broddle, April 2017

Chapter One: Starting Out

"There are two ways of being rich. One is to have all you want. The other is to be satisfied with what you have"

Everyone in our area was either Wednesday or United. You were one or the other. The Blades were my team and I supported them passionately. Most of my mates in our small Yorkshire village were the same. As soon as we were old enough, we would go to see them play as often as we could. We jumped on the local bus from Laughton to Sheffield, paid our 2p fare and headed towards Bramall Lane.

I loved the ground and the atmosphere at the games. I knew all the players and knew everything about the club. When I started to dream about becoming a footballer, Sheffield United were the only team I ever thought about playing for.

Football dominated my childhood from an early age. From as far back as I could remember I would spend my time kicking a ball about on the streets and on the playing fields in our town. I was constantly playing football with friends and even if there was no one else around I'd still be there kicking a ball about on a football pitch or even just against a wall. Football was just what I did. The only thing I ever wanted for Christmas was a new strip or some

football boots or a football. If I received even one of those as a present, I was happy.

It wasn't long before realised I was far better than all my mates. It might sound arrogant but I wasn't at the time. I was just getting on with it and doing what I loved, playing football. Others started to notice my ability too.

Alan Moon and Arthur Bower were two local men who ran Laughton Boys Football Club. They were passionate about the game and had built an incredibly successful team. They instilled in all the boys the right way to play football, as well as the right ethics, principles and common decency to others. One of their teams would eventually earn a place into the Guinness Book of Records, for scoring a ridiculous amount of goals in one season. It was Alan Moon that spotted me kicking a ball about and invited me to be part of the Laughton Boys Football Club. I was only six years old at the time.

It was exciting being asked to be part of the squad. I knew about their brilliant reputation and I knew their team was breaking records. The only trouble was that most of the team were twelve-year olds so I would be playing with the older lads, who were like men to me. I was nervous but thrilled to be given that chance. I was given a place as a substitute at first. Alan wanted to be careful because I was still developing but he wanted to give me experience and I can't thank him enough for the opportunity. He was the person who started it all off for me.

We used to travel to games in an old Transit van that belonged to Alan Moon, and it had two wooden benches in the back for the lads, and we would travel around Yorkshire beating everybody put in front of us. I would do my best to make an impact in games and I was disappointed if I didn't get on the pitch but they used me sparingly which was the right thing to do.

It was my first experience of being part of a football club and I loved every moment of it. You would go to the presentation night at the end of the season. I remember putting on a jumper and a big thick tie to try and look smart and picking up trophies and awards. They were only a little bit of cheap plastic or wood but I still remember the pride I felt getting my first medal.

My parents, Harry and Hilda, weren't as involved in my football as some of the other parents were. They had had me relatively late in life, so both were elderly when I was growing up. It made things difficult when it came to my football. Most parents when they see their son has a chance at becoming a footballer, they go everywhere with them and drive them around to matches.

The age of my parents made this virtually impossible. My father rarely saw me play. I think he only saw me playing in matches about eight or nine times during my entire career. He was always supportive though and after he passed away, his friends told me that he would proudly bring out newspaper cuttings in the pub saying 'our Julian's scored again'.

Aside from their age, my parents were occupied working to provide for our family and looking after my three older brothers, Chris, Kevin and David. My mother was the cook in our local school and my father was the school caretaker. He also had a bit of land next to where we lived and used it to plant vegetables to provide our fresh food. He also used it to grow rhubarb which he sold for an extra bit of income.

We didn't have much money but we wanted for nothing. My parents gave me a good childhood. The one rule was that no one was allowed to swear in our house. My father was very religious and played the organ in our local church for over 40 years. It was his passion and it meant he was well known around the village due to the number of weddings, christenings and funerals he played at. Although my father couldn't get involved in my football as much as a younger parent would have been able to, it didn't hold me back.

In those early days, I always seemed to have a driver. People would want me to play in their team so the manager or the coach would always make the effort to come get me and drop me off back home after the match. The fact that I was so young attracted a lot of attention and it soon got into the local papers that this six-year-old was playing with twelve-year olds. A local businessman called Roy Mugglestone started to take an interest in my talents and somehow persuaded a local TV news programme in Yorkshire, called Calendar, to come to Laughton Junior School to meet me.

My favourite Sheffield United player at the time was Tony Currie. He was an outstanding central midfielder who just strolled around the pitch spraying the ball here, there and everywhere. He had the long hair, the shirt hanging out and he was the celebrity of the team. He later went to play for QPR and Leeds and featured for England a few times. Roy Mugglestone helped arrange for Tony Currie to take part in the filming.

He was my hero and when I met him I was star struck because I wanted to be him. They filmed a few shots of Tony and I meeting, then set up a scenario of me beating several school colleagues and scoring a goal. The TV interviewer then asked me who I wanted to play for when I get old enough. 'Sheffield United' I replied without hesitation. 'And which national team would you like to play for?' he added. I had no idea what a national team was, so repeated proudly, 'Sheffield United'. United was all I was interested in at that point and, although I didn't realise it at the time, would not be long before the club I loved would start to take an interest in my football ability.

Chapter Two: Sheffield United – My Club

"Take risks, if you win, you will be happy, if you lose, you will be wise"

Eddy Edwards was my first proper introduction to Sheffield United. He was a scout for the club and lived in the village around the corner. He knew of the reputation of Laughton Boys and would come to watch our matches regularly. I was eleven years old and it was playing in those matches that he first spotted me. He recognised my talent and recommended me to the club.

He approached me and asked me to sign associated schoolboys with the club. There were no arguments from me. Nottingham Forest, Rotherham United and various other clubs were interested at the time, but to be honest I wouldn't have cared if Liverpool or Manchester United had come in for me at that point. There was only one club for me. It was Sheffield United or nobody.

He came to our house on Remembrance Sunday and met my parents. I signed the forms linking me to the club and it was a very proud moment. I shook his hand and he told me that 'this is just the start'. He was a huge influence on my career in those early years and really guided me. He got dumbbells made for me and would give me an exercise plan and said 'this is how you are going to build yourself up'. He had it all planned out. I was his young star and he expected a lot from me in return. He was always there and was a big part of my young life.

If he was watching when I played games I would feel under pressure. He would obviously praise me if I played well but he wasn't afraid of having a go at me if I'd had a bad game. He used to tell me 'You have to do it Julian. You can't mess about.'

Signing schoolboy forms for the Blades brought with it certain privileges. Nowadays a football club might buy the parents of a promising young player a house to secure their talent, but in those days, all I got was a pass to watch Sheffield United every Saturday. That was more than enough for me. I always used to play on a Saturday morning for the school team, so it was a mad rush to get to Bramall Lane for kick-off.

I would walk up to the player's entrance, show my pass, and in I went. I was just a small kid so I was always worried that they would turn around and say 'Who the hell are you?' but it never happened. I would always hang around for a few minutes to try and see the first team players getting ready for the match. I would walk as slowly as I could near the changing rooms and the tunnel to see if I could catch a glimpse of the players or shake their hand. I sometimes got told to move on but I just wanted to taste a little of what it meant to be a professional footballer in the first team. I wondered whether I would ever get to that level or have the ability.

Then it would be the walk out of the tunnel onto the track around the pitch. My pass allowed me a seat in the stand but I wanted to stand beside my mates. I would head up the tunnel and turn left. It was fantastic and frightening at the same time. There were all these police officers and the huge crowd. I would walk around the side of the football pitch, and walk on the gravel path that took me to the Kop end. I was never sure what to do as I walked past all the supporters waiting for the three o'clock kick off. The noise and atmosphere was amazing. I would walk as quickly as I could and then show my pass to the ground staff who would open a gate to let me in the Kop.

My mates from Laughton always stood in the same place. My main mate was Andy Turner. He was always there for me, and would wind me up about not having to pay to get in, but I knew he was happy for me and wanted me to play for United when I left school. None of my friends ever put me on a pedestal or anything. We just had a laugh and loved watching United.

During that era, United signed an Argentinean named Alex Sabella. Apparently, the club had a lot of scouts in Argentina and the rest of South America. The rumour was that we were going to sign a young talented player called Diego Maradona, but at the last minute someone stepped in and stole him, so the second choice was Sabella. We loved watching him as no one would get near him. He would take two, three, four players on and would go around them with ease.

English football is now full of players from elsewhere, but in those days, everyone was British. Having a foreign player in your team was a real treat. When you went to the games, everyone had cut up bits of newspaper, paper and toilet rolls stuffed in their pockets and as soon as they came out of the tunnel the crowd would throw it towards the pitch to mimic the cascade of paper at the 1978 World Cup in Argentina. It was an incredible experience.

We knew Sabella was too good for us, and eventually he was sold to Leeds United. He didn't settle there and returned to Argentina. At the last World Cup in Brazil, I was astounded to see that the older guy managing the Argentinean national team was none other than Sheffield United's Alex Sabella.

From that moment, I became attached to United as a player my mind was focused on one thing, becoming a professional footballer. I never wanted to be a miner or a bricklayer or an electrician or even make a lot of money. I just wanted to be a footballer and there wasn't a plan B. I didn't work hard enough at school, which I now regret, because in my head I knew I was going to make it as a professional footballer.

Sheffield United wanted me to play for their junior teams. You could either play for a Sheffield team called the Throstles or Worksop Boys club. I opted for Worksop Boys club as they were closer to home. My age group was managed by a lovely man called Brian Howard. He would give me a lift to and from games if Eddy Edwards wasn't around. They trained once a week in the evening and played on Sundays. We had a brilliant team and won everything in our local leagues. I usually played centre midfield and most of the time played well. I had all the confidence in the world then and I felt like I couldn't do anything wrong. I also played for Dinnington High School on a Saturday morning. We had a good team there too and there was a great team spirit as most of the players stayed together during the five years at High school. That became my life for a few years, the school team on Saturdays and Worksop Boys Club on Sundays. When we had school holidays, I would go to Bramall Lane and train there.

As I had a lot of ability in my age group, I also went on to represent Rotherham boys and then South Yorkshire boys. I went along to trials for both of these teams and was fortunate enough to be selected. Rotherham boys trained at Rotherham United's gym at Millmoor in the evenings and sometimes we were lucky to play on the first team football pitch. This would be my first taste of playing at a proper football ground.

The pitch seemed so huge to me with the stands around them. I remember walking onto the pitch and thinking 'This is vast, how am I going to be able to run around here all game?' Even though the stands were empty and there were only a handful of people watching, it gave you a taste of it and I knew I wanted more. I wanted to play at grounds like these in front of thousands of people.

By then, Eddy Edwards had left United and moved to Stoke City, a club flying high in the top division of English football. He had supported me so much as a young player that it was a blow. He did ask me to consider joining him at Stoke, but I couldn't see past Sheffield United. I left Dinnington High School in 1981 after my fifth year. I walked out the school gates on the Friday and arrived at Bramall Lane on the Monday ready to start the next stage of my journey to becoming a professional footballer.

The life of a first-year apprentice at Sheffield United wasn't exactly glamorous. We were immediately set to work painting the walls, scrubbing the kop, cleaning the changing rooms and doing all the horrible jobs apprentices had to do. I think I cleaned every single turnstile of all four sides of the ground. All the apprentices mucked in so it was a good way to get to know some of the other new recruits. There were already second year apprentices at the club who were older, more confident and stronger physically.

They all knew each other and had spent a year together training so it was quite tough group to break into and be accepted as one of the lads. As time went by, they would become great mates, but at first,

I think they saw us as a threat to their place in the junior team or the reserves. You always had that thought at the back of your mind, that your teammates and friends were your biggest rivals to securing a professional contract.

Another responsibility of the apprentices was to look after the senior players by getting their training kit ready and looking after their boots. One of mine was Keith Edwards. He was the big star at the club. He scored more goals than anyone else, even though he rarely left the six-yard area, and he made sure everybody knew he was the top goal scorer. I would try my hardest not to screw up near him but you couldn't avoid getting pelters from him. He used to give me endless stick about my name, Julian being such an unusual name for a footballer at that time. Sometimes the other first team players would catch on to it and they would join in.

Keith was one of the most superstitious footballers I have ever met. He wanted to make sure that everything was done the same way before a game. He even played in the same old battered boots week-in, week-out and when they ripped I had to tape them up and paint them black. He could have had the latest boots from any sponsor in the country because of the number of goals he was scoring but he insisted on wearing his old boots. He didn't change them until it became impossible to keep playing in them.

When I finally turned professional I told him that I no longer had to look after him or clean his boots, but he was so superstitious that he offered me money to keep me on. He was scoring goals for fun when I was his apprentice and he didn't want to change it. I was happy for the additional cash so agreed.

It was at times a harsh environment. At Christmas, it was tradition for the senior players to give you a bonus, but they always made you earn it. You had to sing or run around naked or do something else embarrassing. Some apprentices were even tied up in the middle of the pitch and they fired footballs at them. Can you imagine if they did that now? But that is what they did in those days.

Some of the senior lads who were quieter helped you out and gave you advice, but most of the senior players were too busy living the life of a star footballer and if they thought it was funny to take the piss out of you then they did. It was like years later when I played with Gordon Dalziel. If Dazza could rip the shit out of someone and have banter and fun at their expense then he did it. He would do it to me and he still does it to this day.

You accept it because he is funny, but in those days as a young kid you were just embarrassed and you were scared stiff at times. I worried about what they were going to do to me or say to me so I tried to rush around and get what I needed done and then go back to the safety of the lads my own age.

When I had originally signed for the club, the manager had been the England World Cup legend Martin Peters. He seemed to like me and he came to watch me now and again to play, which I considered a huge honour. To think that this legend that had scored for England in the World Cup would come to watch me play and to take time out to talk to me after the game was an incredible boost to my confidence. Martin Peters left the club to be replaced by Ian Porterfield. Porterfield was still a young man at the time.

He had just gotten Rotherham United promoted so he came to take over Sheffield United when we were in the fourth tier. I was lucky in that Porterfield also liked me and my face seemed to fit. A lot of the time in football it is as much about your face fitting in as it is about your ability.

I was helped by the fact that, as an apprentice, I was allocated responsibility for the manager and his kit. I had to go into his room and get his kit ready and his towel and make it sure it was all clean and dry. I think that helped me develop a stronger relationship with him in those early days. One of the tasks I often got given was cleaning the manager's car. He had this big red car and he always had Elkie Brooks in his cassette player, so myself and a few of the other lads often cleaned his car with 'Pearl is a Singer' blasting in the background.

There were some great characters at Sheffield United in that era. Keith Edwards was the star striker and he was joined by big personalities like sweeper Tony Kenworthy and John McPhail, a strong centre-half from Scotland. Tony was one of those guys who always had the latest hairstyles, always looked good and always smelt nice. He had this beautiful white VW Golf and his girlfriend looked like a Miss World contestant.

John was a big, strong guy with piercing blue eyes and that no nonsense Scottish accent. You never argued with him. These guys were always in the local nightclubs and were the heart of the club. At the time, you looked up to the first team players. They were what you aspired to be. You hoped that maybe one day you might be training with them and be their teammate.

Every Friday, Ian Porterfield would put the team lists up on this board and everybody would pile around to see if they were in the first team squad or playing in the juniors. After a short time, Ian Porterfield put me into the reserves.

When you played for the Sheffield United junior team, you played in the Northern Intermediate League made up of most of the North of England teams. All the players were young and just starting out. Sheffield United Reserves was a whole different experience. We played in the Central League, and the squads were usually made up mostly of senior players that were coming back from injury or first team substitutes needing game time, with the odd young player moving up from the junior team like myself.

We were playing at Old Trafford, Anfield, Villa Park and you would go on these nice big buses to the games. I remember playing Manchester United reserves at Old Trafford once and there was five and a half thousand there. That was the biggest crowd I had ever played in front of.

I soon realised that I was playing with grown men and it was a massive step-up. There were often a lot of disgruntled senior players in the dressing room at times as they had fallen out of the manager's plans. One week, Sheffield United first team had had a terrible result on the Saturday so the manager dropped a lot of the regulars into the reserves as a punishment. A few players could be very negative and would moan for Britain about having to travel to a midweek reserve match at Bolton, but most had a brilliant attitude, as they fought to get back into the first team or get a move elsewhere. You were also playing against some famous senior players from other teams who were in the reserves or coming back from injury. It was great to be involved with the senior players who had seen it all done it all in their careers and I remember being up against Howard Kendall in one match against Everton.

I once also played against Mark Walters, who would later go on to sign for Glasgow Rangers. I was given the task of marking him. I was fast in those days but the speed he had was frightening. He was like lightning. I didn't know what had hit me. I was left standing there thinking 'How am I ever going to be able to cope with this?' But thankfully not every player I came up against had the skills and pace of Mark Walters.

A favourite memory was nutmegging a very senior Manchester United player who I shall not name. He didn't take to kindly to it and angrily warned me 'If you ever do that again, I will break your legs'.

When I was around sixteen I was doing so well that I got called to England trials. I was nervous but excited, as it was a huge honour at the time. My mum had bought me this maroon velvet suit from the local store in Rotherham, so that I would look smart. I'm not sure how ridiculous I looked like at the time but in those days, I didn't know any different. I travelled down on the train to the England camp at Lilleshall with Paul Stewart, who would later go on to play for Tottenham Hotspur.

I was there a couple of days and then I received the news that Ian Porterfield wanted me to return to Sheffield to be in the squad. Who knows how the rest of the trials would have turned out but when the manager says he wants you back, you have to go back.

Life off the field at the time was great too. I had left home and moved into a house that belonged to United. The house was mainly for young players who lived a distance from home. We were looked after by an elderly couple in an area called Nether Edge in Sheffield. It was a lovely tree lined road and it was massive. They had built a modern extension on the side and that is where all the young apprentices lived.

They looked after us incredibly well, they cooked for us and cleaned up after us and made sure that we had what we needed. Every so often you would get one of the senior players staying. If they signed a player and he didn't have accommodation yet then he would come and stay with us for a few days until they got him sorted or he rented a house.

I was placed in room two with a lad called Richard Cooper who had come from Lincolnshire. He was quite a chilled, laid back guy and we became best of friends. It was just a house full of young lads and you would come back from training and hang out. Occasionally you would go out into town to go shopping or for a beer, but we didn't have much money in those days so most days we just hung around or watched television. I remember watching a lot of snooker when the World Championships were on. It was a really easy-going place and the doors were never locked, people just came and went.

Security was so relaxed that one night I woke up at 3am in the morning to find seven or eight teenage girls in our room. They were all dressed up and wearing make-up. I wasn't sure whether I was dreaming or not at first but then I realised that this was actually happening.

My roommate Richard Cooper then woke up and started screaming at them to get out just in case they would get us into trouble. I sat there confused with part of me naively thinking 'Hold on Coops, don't be so hasty, one of these girls could turn out to be my first girlfriend'. He quickly chased them out though. We found out later they all from a care home nearby which looked after young people who had experienced difficulties in their lives. They had found out that there was a house full of Sheffield United footballers in the area and had decided to explore.

We had some great times in that house. I loved living there. I think a few of the other lads from Wales or further away may have got a bit homesick at times but as a local lad, I knew I could hop on a bus and be home in thirty minutes if I wanted to. There was a great togetherness in the group when we played together but there was also a lot of rivalry and jealousy.

We all had the same goal, trying to make it as professional footballers and in training the tackles were ridiculous, no one held back. Sometimes we trained with the first team to help them get ready for a match and we were soon told by the manager not to tackle as fiercely as we did amongst ourselves just in case we injured the senior players.

Ian Porterfield was brilliant. He came along with all these new ideas and the training was fantastic. We would do this huge circle warm-up and just jumping up and down to different rhythms. We would then act as the opposition to the first team squad. Sometimes the athlete Sebastian Coe used to come and train and run with us. He would go on to win Olympic Gold but in those days, he was obviously just looking for a bit of extra training.

The club sent all the apprentices to a local college to do a media course. We joined the Sheffield Wednesday lads on this course to try and teach us about how to communicate and be confident in front of the cameras, how to do interviews and stuff like that. I think we were probably the first generation of players to do that. It was there that I met my first proper girlfriend. I met Caroline, who as at that college who was one year older and we were together for two and a half years in the end.

My Dad bought a little mini for £100 from our village and I used to go and pick her up in that. It was a little blue wreck but I adored it. There were holes in the floor and you had to lift the door up to shut it. I remember once we were driving along a road towards Sheffield City Centre and the police stopped me. He asked me who I was and where I was going. I answered him and then he asked what I did for a living. I told him I was a footballer at Sheffield United. He looked at me confused and said 'You're a footballer? How come you've got a car like this, it's not even bloody roadworthy!' I lied through my teeth and told them that I was only using it temporarily as I was waiting on a brand-new Golf GTi being delivered. Thankfully they were United fans so they let me off!

I kept my place in the reserves and even managed to score the odd goal, so I gained a tremendous amount of experience in that first several months. Within a year I was signing a professional contract.

Chapter Three: Making my Debut

"People know you for what you have done, not for what you plan to do"

From the moment, I thought about playing football professionally, everything was focused on Sheffield United. Many may dream of making it to the top of the game and featuring for Manchester United, Barcelona or Real Madrid, but for me it was only ever about turning out for the Blades. January 2nd 1982 was to be the day I fulfilled my ambitions and made my senior football debut for Sheffield United.

I had no idea that I would be playing so my preparation for the match wasn't exactly ideal. I had spent New Year's Eve out all night at a house party getting drunk with some of my Sheffield United mates. It was during that party, that someone pushed the Sheffield Star newspaper in my face, with the headline that Julian Broddle is in the squad to play against Halifax Town and may make his debut.

I was shocked at the time seeing my name in the local paper but I just thought the manager would have me warming the bench to give me some experience. Never in my wildest dreams did I think I would actually be selected to start. After the party, I remember walking halfway across Sheffield in the early hours of New Year's Day, to get home. In those days, there was no way I would pay for a taxi but thankfully I was fit enough to do it.

The day of the game arrived. It was cold, wet, dark and miserable, and I was sat in the corner of the dressing room hoping the boss would make me at least a sub for the day. He read out the team and reached my name. I was in, playing left midfield. I didn't know what to do. Immediately the nerves kicked in. I was just a young boy amongst all these grown men. The senior players were coming up to me and shaking my hand and telling me not to worry. They were advising me on what to do and telling me just to enjoy myself. I wasn't really listening to be honest because I was so stressed out.

I knew I had to tell my parents, so Dad could be there to see his son play for the Blades. Once I had got the news to him, I then started to get changed from my suit to the first team strip. I had dreamed all my life to wear the Red Black and White kit, and now I was one hour from running onto the Bramall Lane pitch in front of thousands of fans. I knew that my Dad would be there and all my mates would be there. I was proud but I was mostly thinking 'don't mess up'. I just didn't want to make a mistake.

It was very quickly time to go down the tunnel and run onto the pitch to the roar of the crowd. As I emerged from the tunnel I looked around and tried to take in the crowd noise, the size of the ground and everything about the occasion. It was difficult as I was mostly thinking 'what am I doing here?' In my head, I wasn't sure I was deserving of my place and didn't feel like I should be there. I was totally unprepared and I wasn't ready.

The game kicked off and my legs were like jelly. When I got the ball, I thought best to just keep everything simple and pass the ball to my colleagues. The game went quickly and I couldn't get my head around just how fast the pace was. I just wasn't used to the speed coming from junior and reserve football. It wasn't helped by the fact that it was an atrocious day and the pitch was terrible. The Bramall Lane pitch was terrible in those days, a proper mud bath and this day was no different. The game passed me by. I can't remember anything about it. All I remember is that we didn't play that well and drew 2-2.

At the time, I wasn't aware of it but I became the youngest player to feature for Sheffield United in their one-hundred-year history. When I look back on that now I am incredibly proud of that achievement. To think that there is this big club with a great history and at that point, I was their youngest ever player was fantastic.

I knew I didn't play particularly well and was totally shattered during and after the game, but under the circumstances, as the pitch was poor, and it was so cold and damp, I didn't want to berate myself too much. I got showered after the game and went

home, and looked forward to seeing how the evening sport paper would write about the match and what they would say about me. I bought the paper and could see that there was a picture of me taken during the game. I had my shirt out of my shorts and I looked like a dishevelled kid. The words underneath the picture said, "BRODDLE WILL GET ANOTHER CHANCE."

I enjoyed several days of extra attention after my debut and I can now readily admit, enjoyed the limelight. No one from my area had ever played for Sheffield United so it was a proud moment and I enjoyed the tiny bit of celebrity that came my way. It was after that I gained confidence and that is where things started to go wrong. I started to think that I should be in the squad every week. Reflecting on it now, I think my ego got too big over the next few weeks. I kept getting into the squad but no further. As time went by, I got frustrated because I thought I was good enough to feature in the first team.

My situation wasn't helped by the purchase of Jeff King from Sheffield Wednesday as a left midfielder. King was a total Scottish eccentric, full of energy and hyperactive. He would often sleep in his car when he couldn't get into his marital home, and he would often be found in snooker clubs playing on his own, as he had nowhere to go! As a player, he was very slight in build and a busy player, always winning penalties.   I suddenly became third choice behind King and Steve Charles. Steve Charles was a super fit, intelligent local lad, who was great player. I realised I would struggle to get my second chance.

I decided to voice my frustration to the manager. I went to see Ian Porterfield in his huge office. I was so frightened when knocking on his door and I was shaking like a leaf. By then, Scunthorpe had taken an interest in me and I think in my head I hoped that he would see that another team were interested and say 'ok son, we don't want to lose you so I will give me some more opportunities in the first team'. He didn't. He told me that he had already given me a chance and that if I wanted another I needed to work hard to earn it. I was dumbstruck.

I left his office with the offer from Scunthorpe ringing in my ears. I knew the chief scout at Scunthorpe, Eddy Edwards, very well as he had had scouted me for Sheffield United as an 11-year-old. Eddy kept telling me that I would get a chance at Scunthorpe and I could progress. I went home to think about the offer from Scunthorpe and decided to accept I had no choice but to say yes. I think I had gotten too big for my boots, and thought it would be better playing more often for their first team rather than never getting that second game for United.

At the time Scunthorpe were in the same division as the Blades, so it didn't feel like a backwards move. I think I had in my head that I would get regular football with Scunthorpe and would return to Sheffield United a season or so later for money, and receive a hero's welcome.

Leaving Sheffield United was hard. The club had been all I had ever known. I had grown up with them. They were my life. I was devastated. I was also leaving behind a lot of good friends. Looking back now, I do have regrets. Playing for Sheffield United was the one thing I wanted to do and I did it. I am immensely proud of that, but I would love to be able to say that I played thirty games for Sheffield United, not just one. A few months ago, I was a guest at Scunthorpe United when they played Sheffield United. I went on the pitch and most of the Scunthorpe supporters knew who I was. The Sheffield United end didn't have a clue.

I suppose that is a disappointment, that I didn't make more of a mark and didn't play enough games to be recognised by the fans of the club I love. But I did play for them and I think the older I get, the more I appreciate that fact. Most supporters would love to have featured in their side's first team. I got that opportunity and it is something I will treasure. I left Bramall Lane with a heavy heart but I knew that I had to focus on my new challenge, establishing myself as a Scunthorpe player.

Chapter Four:
Scunthorpe United

"Every path has a few puddles"

I arrived at Scunthorpe and was immediately struck by how different it was to Sheffield United. United had this massive stadium and Scunthorpe was, well let's just say it wasn't the best stadium in the world. The stadium, the crowd, the atmosphere was just different. It was a totally different way of thinking. It was more like a local social club football team at times.

When I arrived, and looked around the Old Show Ground, it was very hard not to think, 'What have I done?' The stadium was small and very run down and the changing rooms were from the Victorian days! Sheffield United had just built a new stand with fantastic changing rooms and facilities, and here I was cramped into a tiny changing room with a mix of free transfer players and local lads who I didn't know.

Moving to a new club was always unsettling for me, right through my career. I always walked through the doors of a new club thinking 'will they like me? Will they slag me off about my name? Will they give me pelters about the way I look? I had this stupid name Julian and then with the way I looked with these big blue eyes, I was always worried about getting stick.

If you knew someone at the club that would be a huge help as you could latch onto them but I never lost that nervousness when I walked into a dressing room for the first time. That never changed throughout my time as a footballer and even carried on into my police career. I was always nervous going into a new team. It was something that followed me around.

There was also an added pressure on me having been brought to the club to make a difference. The club expected more from me. I had been brought along to play on a regular basis. I was expected to enhance their team. They had looked at me and thought 'there's a young lad at Sheffield United. Let's have him and hopefully he can do the business for us'. The one good thing about Scunthorpe United was that I knew Eddy Edwards and Geoff Day, who had left Sheffield United to join Scunthorpe at the same time as me. They helped me eventually settle in.

The Manager was the ex-Leeds and England legend, Allan Clarke. The new boss was a very confident, slim, tall well-dressed man. He had a superb career as a footballer and truly believed in his managerial abilities. Although he would later become a very good friend, at first, I found him very intimidating and couldn't work him out. I was still just a young lad starting out in the game. Allan Clarke worshipped Don Revie from his Leeds days. His belief was that if it was good enough for Leeds

United then it was good enough for Scunthorpe Football Club. This extended to making sure we all had to drink this shot of whisky before a game. Some of the lads never even touched alcohol, never mind whisky but we all had to take a drink. It was a tradition at Leeds so he brought it to Scunthorpe.

I made my debut for Scunthorpe at Port Vale away. It was a massive pitch and I didn't play well at all. We secured a draw but because of my poor performance, I started to worry that I just didn't have what it took to make it as a footballer. I thought I've played for Sheffield United and didn't do anything for them on my debut and now my Scunthorpe United debut has been average. For the first time, I started to think that I might not make it. I knew Sheffield United was a big team and if you left them then you could always go down the leagues.

I suddenly had that feeling that if I left Scunthorpe, where would I go? Probably out of the game. I knew I hadn't stuck in at school so trying to find something else to do with my life became a concern. At the time, I was also finding it hard to move on from Sheffield United. I was still thinking about them. I missed all my good mates, whereas at Scunthorpe I felt like I was out on my own.

My problem throughout my entire career was my head. If I wasn't mentally strong then I didn't perform. If my manager loved the bones of me then it gave me confidence and I played well. If I played well then it gave me more confidence and I kicked on and played well again. When I had a bad game then it started to affect me psychologically and I might dip for three games.

If I could go back now I would make sure that mental attitude would be totally different but it was all about the head with me. If I had a manager that put his arms around me and told me what a great player I was or gave me confidence then it was great, but if a manager wanted to kick me up the arse of have a go at me it never worked for me. I had only very short periods in my 17-year career where when I played; I was playing at the top of my game and felt I could beat anybody.

The first season at Scunthorpe I was in an out and it was hard going. I was always struggling. I was up and down and very unpredictable. I was always worried about whether I was going to be dropped or not. It wasn't just my football career that I was worried about, the financial side of things also mattered. We didn't get paid much money in those days so if you got appearance money, even just as a substitute then it helped you pay your mortgage and pay your bills. I had married my first wife Jan and we had bought our first house.

The story of how we got together was an unusual one. We had met on a school trip to Italy as children and had started writing to each other. Years later when I was on a trip to Liverpool with a mate, I thought 'stuff this, why don't I go and see Jan?', so I drove to her area and that was that. We were inseparable and later married.

The story of our meeting intrigued many and even won us a national competition. The year that Prince Andrew and Sarah Ferguson got married TVAM ran  a competition looking for the most romantic story.
Unbeknown to me, Jan had sent the story of how we got together into this competition.
She talked about how we wrote to each other since we were 11 years old and how she had kept every letter and now we were getting married. They narrowed it down to the last four couples and then we got a phone call saying we had won. We went to the TVAM studios in a chauffeur driven car and were interviewed about our wedding and the thoughts on the Royal Wedding. We received a lot of perks and we got to hang around the studios and meet other people who were on the show like Roger Daltry. I was so nervous being interviewed on live television sat there in a bright yellow jumper. Thankfully I was fortunate, because it was on so early in the morning the lads at Scunthorpe never saw it. If they had, then

life in the dressing room wouldn't have been worth living!

A memorable moment for me was my first League goal. We were due to play Sheffield United at Bramall Lane in a midweek game on November 1st, 1983. It would be a great occasion back playing at Bramall Lane and under the floodlights, especially because it also happened to be my birthday. I was desperate to play, and I think Allan Clarke knew this, and put me in the team. We had a small squad at Scunthorpe and the manager knew I was quick and I think he realised that I would be especially motivated playing against my old club and put me upfront. It was strange to be back at Bramall Lane, back at 'my club' and finding myself in the away dressing room.

United were flying at the time and we were struggling in the league. My friends and family were there again and watched the Blades beat us 5-3, with Keith Edwards scoring the goals to defeat us. Although we had lost, it was a great night as I had managed to score my very first senior goal. As a child growing up I had always dreamed of scoring at Bramall Lane, but I'd always assumed that it be for Sheffield United, not against them.

I scored at the away end with my right foot against my old teammate Keith Waugh and I turned away after scoring and wasn't sure what to do. I was delighted to have scored but it was mixed with a degree of sadness about who it was against. Regardless, it became a birthday that I would never forget. It was an amazing thing to go back and do that and I now had my first goal and hoped that there were many more to come.

During my early time at Scunthorpe, I had the terrible heartache of losing one of my best friends, Andrew Turner. I was travelling back from the south after a game, and I got the news that Andy, who came from my home village, Laughton, had passed away. He was only a young man and he worked in the local mine and had died from a very rare disease that affects only 4 people every year in the U.K. I always remember Andy telling me when we were younger that he was going to die young, that he had a feeling. I told him to stop being crazy and not talk like that, but he was proven right. In that same chat, he told me that he was disappointed that I had left Sheffield United but I must keep going and get up the leagues.

I asked the manager Allan Clarke for time off for the funeral but the boss told me that we were short of players and I was required for an important game, so couldn't go. At the time, I was shocked and angry, but I was a very young player at the time and I couldn't tell the manager where to go so instead, my parents went to the funeral to represent me. Andy was buried in his beloved Sheffield United jumper and badge and too this day I often visit his grave for a chat. Andy was a great guy and a true Blade and he would have the first to give me stick for scoring against his beloved team.

The manager at Scunthorpe changed from Al

Ian Clarke to Frank Barlow. Frank was a lovely guy and another former Blade. I was fast in those days and spent most of my time either up front or on the left win. We got a good team together and I started gaining more confidence and experience. Things started to click and I scored quite a lot of goals. I remember one particular season scoring the fastest goal of the year in the entire Football League, netting after just 10 seconds against Southend United. We kicked off and they didn't touch the ball before I put the ball in the back of the net!

A highlight of my Scunthorpe days was getting to know and play alongside legendary England cricketer Ian Botham. 'Beefy' was a great character and a sporting superstar at the time. He was at the height of his brilliant cricketing exploits, and wherever he went, the media went. It was fascinating having him as one of the lads. We played him as a centre half but I think he always wanted to be played upfront. He was not a bad centre half and when he played, it always drew more of a crowd

I remember in the early days when we were training, he would be throwing up halfway round the pitch as he wasn't used to that intensity of training and fitness. We used to slaughter him. One winter all the lads attacked him with snowballs and buried him in a pile of snow. He loved it. He just wanted to be treated like one of the lads. Before one match he disappeared and Alan Clark couldn't find him so he sent me to look for him. I found him in the changing room toilet, sat in the cubicle with the door half open. He had a cigar in his mouth, a shot of whisky next to him and he was engrossed reading the programme for that day. What a sight.

At Christmas, the lads would go on a Christmas piss up around the pubs in outer Scunthorpe and then into town. Incredibly, all of it was paid for by Ian, including the van to take us from pub to pub. He had to have a minder because of press interest in him so his minder would drive the van and take care of us in case any of the locals wanted a fight. He was a great guy, really down to earth and he wanted to be an ambassador for Scunthorpe Football Club.

Years later, I remember playing for Barnsley, away at Sunderland. We sneaked a draw and after the match while I was getting changed, there was a knock at the door of the dressing room. The door opened and there was Beefy Botham wanting me to meet him in the players bar for a beer. The rest of the Barnsley lads were stunned. My teammate Mark Robinson later said to me, "I cannot believe it, Ian Botham is my hero and he's knocking on the door to ask you to meet him in the bar!" I met him in the bar and had a few beers and then had to get on the coach to make our way back to Barnsley. I'm proud that I had the chance to have such great memories with a living legend.

During my years in the professional game, I was lucky enough to rarely get injured. I never got any breaks or anything too serious. While at Scunthorpe, I got some dirt in an open cut and over a few days the cut on the inside of my left knee got infected and

became an abscess. It blew up to the size of a golf ball. The club's physio, Phil McLoughlin was a bit of a character who didn't mess around when trying to get you back to fitness. Phil had asked me into his room and I laid down on one of the two treatment tables. We were chatting away and looking at the injury and strangely, I noticed some of the lads started hovering around.

They were usually showered and off home as quickly as they could after training. Suddenly, the lads, about five of them, grabbed onto my legs and upper body and forced me down hard to the table. Phil then went over to something was boiling away in the corner of the room and took out what could only be referred to as a branding iron. He took the brander and pushed it hard against my leg and held it there for what felt like a lifetime. I could hear the sound of it sizzling as I screamed my head off. Thankfully, it did the trick, so thanks lads.

During the Frank Barlow era, we just missed out by a point to get in the playoffs in the 1984- 1985 season. We went on a brilliant run where we were scoring goals for fun. We beat Swindon 6-2, Tranmere Rovers 5-2 and poor old Exeter 7-1. We were flying and it was frustrating just not quite getting into the play offs, as I truly believe we would have got promoted had we had done so.

I was young and super fit and fast and my pace kept me away from the tough defenders. Frank Barlow later told me there were a few big clubs looking at me, and I thought it was a matter of time before I got that chance, but for some reason, it never happened. I scored every round of our FA Cup run one year and we got through to the fifth round to play Tottenham at White Hart Lane. I always remember the headline at the time 'Hoddle, Waddle and Broddle'. I may have been last in the list but it was great to even be mentioned alongside great players of that calibre. I was told that Tottenham were interested in signing me after that but the clubs couldn't come to an arrangement. Our Chairman apparently said no and that was that. Someone also told me that Manchester United were looking at me. I would love to know about what went wrong when clubs put offers in for me. I know they did, but either Scunthorpe was wanting too much or the other clubs were just not prepared to pay over the odds. This was the era before television and money was tight. I was playing really well in a small team, but I knew I wanted to get higher up. Don't get me wrong, I had some fantastic times at Scunthorpe and the fans treated me so well. But I knew I had the ability to go higher. But every time someone was rumoured to be interested I would have a bit of dip in form so the big move I was after never happened. They probably thought that I was too unpredictable.

This was the terrible era of the miners' strike. As a footballer, I was somewhat protected from the worst of that time but it was rough for a lot of my friends from my home village and surrounding area. I was aware of the situation and watched on television as the strike unfolded. Our area was a strong mining community and Orgreave Colliery was close to my home. I would travel the 36 miles from Scunthorpe from Laughton and back.

There were a few of us living in the Sheffield area, so we would meet up and take it in turns to do the journey and save money. We were young lads not earning much and so our cars reflected this. My car was a black Triumph Dolomite sport, and I can remember Geoff Day had an old Vauxhall Viva. It didn't take long before we got stopped by the Police thinking we were flying pickets. When we told the Police, we were footballers they let us go.

My time at Scunthorpe came to an end when Mick Buxton arrived as manager. Buxton was from Huddersfield, and was a very tough, hard

Yorkshireman. It wasn't until later in my career that I realised when tough managers took over at the clubs I played for, I usually was out of the door fairly quickly. I had been training during the summer period to keep reasonably fit, thinking that when Buxton arrived, that he would be impressed by my actions. In my era, it was usual to just go away and get away from football entirely, and enjoy your time off. Most managers would tell you to go and relax and forget about football and re charge the batteries. This would usually include drinking alcohol to the extreme.

Buxton didn't like me and I felt it immediately. I only played a few games for him and played alright so I don't know why he didn't want me as a player. I was probably one of the better players at the club but my face just didn't fit. Maybe Buxton thought I would be arrogant and decided to stamp his authority or perhaps I didn't jump through hoops and run through walls for him. I never really clicked with managers who were hard as nails. However, I was soon on the subs bench at the beginning of the season and going nowhere fast. I knew it was time to move on.

We were doing a photo shoot for the local paper regarding the soon to be built new stadium, Glanford Park. It was the first stadium to be built after all the terrible disasters at Bradford and Hillsborough. We had the team picture taken by a large JCB digger. As soon as it was over, I drove over to Barnsley football Club, who were in the then second tier, to have talks with their manager, my old friend Allan Clarke.

Allan was there with Frank Barlow and Eddy Edward and I knew that at least they believed in me. I agreed a contract with Barnsley and later found out that Scunthorpe sold me for only £10,000.

There was uproar in the local papers and even the local MP got involved. People didn't understand why Mick Buxton was getting rid of a player who was an asset and who may have earned the club a significant transfer fee. I think the fact that I went to Barnsley, a club in the local area made the supporters even more upset. After the move, I lived in Scunthorpe for a while until I sold my house.

I could not help but smile to myself when I saw the local Scunthorpe paper getting letters from fans, furious that they had sold off their best player so cheaply, and fans would often come up to me thanking me for my time at the club and saying they missed my attacking abilities! I'd loved my time at Scunthorpe and the fans but Barnsley wanted me and clearly the management at Scunthorpe didn't.

Chapter Five: Barnsley AFC

"I am not here to change the world. I am changing the world because I am here"

I joined Barnsley in 1987. It was a big step up. I was playing two divisions higher than I had been with Scunthorpe and we had a number of massive clubs in our division, including Manchester City, Newcastle United, Leeds United and my old club, Sheffield United. It was a tough league.

Settling in at Barnsley was easier than most of my other clubs as I knew Allan Clarke and Frank Barlow and I was lucky to travel in with another player called Jim Dobbin, which helped ease me into the Barnsley dressing room. I used to pick Jim up in Doncaster on my way through from Scunthorpe and we shared the petrol costs. It was helpful to chat to an established player every day and the knowledge he had about the club was invaluable. Jim was a bit of a character. He was originally from Scotland but had settled in Doncaster having previously playing for Doncaster Rovers. He was always up to no good and constantly playing tricks in the dressing room.

We were playing a head tennis game between a few of us at training one day when Jim came running over and couldn't stop laughing. He was almost in tears. He told us he had put a lot of knots in Allan

Clarke's training bottoms which apparently left the manager sweating buckets for thirty minutes trying to get them out. The manager arrived late into the training ground looking a little hot and bothered.

When I looked down at the gaffer's training gear, I saw the most creased up bottoms I had ever seen. Jim also made a habit of standing naked or semi-naked in front of the parents or grandparents of the mascot as he was shown round the dressing room. I'm sure there was more than one home video of the young mascot walking around the dressing room getting his programme signed which features Jim in the background bent over in briefs or naked!

He would also put deep heat on his hands and when he shook the kid's or parent's hands, the deep heat would rub off. You can just imagine the poor kid later rubbing his eyes with deep heat on his hands. Cruel!

Jim helped me settle into life at Barnsley. The approach to the game at Barnsley was very different to what I had been used to. At Scunthorpe, they would knock it over the top and I could use my pace to chase it down. Barnsley refused to knock it long. You had to pass it all the time.

The manager Allan Clarke was still using some of his Leeds United traditions that he had taken to Scunthorpe United. We always played bingo on away trips with the winner forced to be the compere for the next game. I still recall the sight of all the lads, in bright red tracksuits, playing bingo at some fancy hotel. He also wanted to make sure the squad had massages, followed by a cold bath then hot bath, another Leeds United tradition. The tradition that worked best for me was the Friday before a Saturday match. The training was a warm up then a very quick five a side then finished. I clearly wasn't a very enthusiastic trainer!

Allan Clarke always drummed into us how lucky we were to be playing football for a living. He was really good in the community, getting the team out and about and seen. He would take us down the mines or a carpet factory and say to us, 'this is what you could be doing. These lads are working all hours and they don't get much and they come on a Saturday to watch you. So, appreciate what you have.' That made all of us reflect on what we could have been doing if we hadn't have been blessed with the ability to play football. It pushed me and the rest of the squad on to be the best that you could be.

As for the football, I started as a substitute at first, getting on for the last twenty minutes or so in the first few games. When I did get my chance, I played ok but was nothing special at first. I was playing left wing and probably needed to be fitter. I struggled a bit with calf problems and I used to cramp up every now and again. Now, with hindsight it was because I never drank enough water and ate a lot of bread. If only I could go back with the knowledge and insight I have now and play again. I'm sure I would be fitter and faster!

Barnsley played brilliant football. It was all pass, pass, pass and at times, it was a pleasure to watch. We had a local lad called Steve Agnew and a Welsh lad, Gwyn Thomas in centre midfield, and they kept buzzing around passing and moving. Stuart Gray played either midfield or in defence and he just oozed class. Stuart had played for Nottingham Forest. He went about his game professionally and quietly and it was such a shame that he would always pick up injuries. Former Manchester City player Paul Futcher was at the back. He was coming towards the end of his career, but he still had the quality of someone who had played at the highest level. Up front was the hard-working pair of Rodger

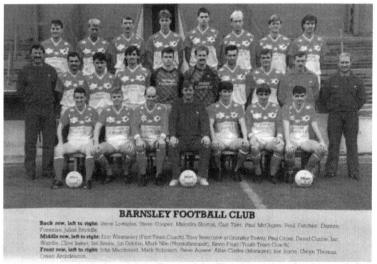

BARNSLEY FOOTBALL CLUB

Back row, left to right: Steve Lowndes, Steve Cooper, Malcolm Shotton, Carl Tiler, Paul McCrystal, Paul Futcher, Darren Foreman, Julian Broddle.
Middle row, left to right: Eric Winstanley (First Team Coach), Tony Rees (now at Grimsby Town), Paul Cross, David Currie, Ian Wardle, Clive Baker, Ian Banks, Jim Dobbin, Mark Nile (Physiotherapist), Kevin Fogg (Youth Team Coach).
Front row, left to right: John MacDonald, Mark Robinson, Steve Agnew, Allan Clarke (Manager), Joe Joyce, Gwyn Thomas, Owen Archdeacon.

Wylde and John MacDonald. Rodger had played for a few clubs, including Sheffield Wednesday and was a class act, a really lovely man.

John McDonald had played for Glasgow Rangers, and like all strikers need to be, was very confident of his own ability. He used his small stature to get in about the defence, nipping at their legs and bugging them and mostly scoring from inside the six-yard box. The captain of Barnsley was Joe Joyce. Joe was an athlete who had spent most of his career at Barnsley. He was super fit, played the simple game and tough in the tackle at right back.

The two main players on my side of the field were Paul Cross and John Beresford. Paul would become my rival for the left side and he had a no-nonsense game, and never let the team down. John Beresford was a popular left midfielder at the club. It was his transfer to Portsmouth that really opened up an opportunity for me to make my mark at the club.

I was helped by the fact that the fans were completely behind me. At Barnsley if you don't get stuck in, work hard and prove yourself then the fans let you know. They don't hold back. If you are rubbish they will tell you that you are rubbish. Thankfully the fans were good to me. I remember once after we lost I was in the B&Q on a Sunday and a Barnsley fan came up to me. 'Barnsley were bloody rubbish yesterday' he said, before adding 'but you're alright, you played alright and you're not a bad bloody player you.' The fans never gave me any stick at all. They were a great support.

They also backed the team magnificently. I remember a two-legged League Cup match in against West Ham United. The first leg was at home and had ended goalless. We travelled to Upton Park to face a West Ham team full of quality players like Paul Ince, Tony Cottee, Alvin Martin and the brilliant Liam Brady. There was a great atmosphere under the floodlights with a vast army of Barnsley fans making the journey.

We started slowly and found ourselves two goals down to a West Ham side playing total football. We were a powerful team though and even when it looked like we had lost the game, we would continue to push forward. We staged an incredible fightback to win 5-2. It was an amazing game, and as the game went by, my confidence grew and along with rest of my teammates I got better and better. It was an honour to play my part in a match Barnsley fans still fondly remember to this day.

I also remember an FA Cup tie against Bolton, when I managed to score two goals. The Manager played me up front sometimes and I would work hard running either side, holding up the ball. When I did get my chance in front of the goals, I usually took it and scored. I loved that moment, as years after, when I became a Police officer; I worked in Bolton for a few years and would tease my Bolton supporting colleagues with my story of knocking them out of the FA cup. It always kept them quiet!

We had some great games against our Yorkshire rivals Leeds United. They were real scraps with large, boisterous crowds. At one of these games I encountered the Leeds centre half Noel Blake. He was a huge, scary character and didn't like losing. It was a fast and furious game in front of a full house but we were doing well and I was causing Leeds trouble running up and down the left side of the pitch at pace. I was flying down the left wing, when I saw Noel Blake running over to take me out. He reached me a second late and I went tumbling to the ground into the advertising boards. The ref came over to Blake and immediately showed him the red card. Before he walked off, Blake came over to me and towered over me as I lay on the ground. He looked straight into my eyes and said 'I will get you for this, and I don't care how long it takes.' At the time, I didn't care and responded with a shrug and a look that said 'whatever'. After his sending off we went on to win the game so I quickly forget about Noel Blake. He was less quick to forget the incident, although it would take until I moved to Scotland for his chance of revenge.

Allan Clarke moved me to left back when Paul Cross got a bad injury. This gave me the opportunity to get established there, and I started off really well and continued to get better. I hardly missed a game and loved my football. I always used to look at what my rating was in the Sunday paper. You looked to see if you got a seven, an eight or a nine or whether you were nominated star man. I was getting good ratings and praise in the match reports and my confidence was sky high.

I kept my place for the rest of the season and into the next season at left back as Paul was still recovering from his serious leg injury. I knew at some point, he would be fit, but I was playing so well, I thought he would struggle to get his place back from me. We played Ipswich away on the very

first match of the season. I had a great game and Paul made a point of coming over to me and telling me how well I was playing and that he thought he wouldn't get in when fit. That's nice to hear from your colleague and rival to the same position.

Eventually Paul cross did get fit and I thought, let battle commence. Incredibly, just as a decision from the manager needed to be made, our right back Joe Joyce got a bad injury. Paul Cross was all left footed so it was yours truly who ended up at right back! I do have a right foot and could use it to a degree but it was always going to be difficult having never played on the right side. I played there for six months and never once got dropped so I suppose I must have done something right.

The hardest opponent I came up against in that position was in a game against Leeds United. My task was to keep Gordon Strachan quiet. Strachan is a very clever player and played on the fact I am mainly a left footed player. He played well and gave me a torrid time. He has a very clever brain and was always two steps ahead of me, so I was glad to hear the final whistle. He was always a difficult opponent. I played against him at Leeds United and Manchester United and he never failed to give me a tough time, even when I was in my natural position on the left.

One season we just missed out on a play-off place by one point to Swindon Town. We went on a great run near the end of the season and were playing some fantastic football at the time. We were the form team in the division but just ran out of games, otherwise, I am convinced we would have gone on to impress in the play-off matches and secure promotion to the top league.

Life at the time was brilliant. I was playing well at a good level, getting ok money with a good bunch of lads. I got the recognition in the papers and it was just down the road from where I lived. Everything was good about it and everything was going well. It was a really nice part of my life and football career. At the time, I even bought the local milk rounds in

Laughton to show I wanted to be part of our village and the community and give something back.

The club bought a player from Darlington called David Currie for £160,000. Dave played up front and as soon as he joined, he scored goals for fun. He became my roommate when staying in hotels and like most forwards, was very cocky and confident. Every day, Dave Currie would turn up looking like a tramp and he had the hair to go with it. He used to wear these moccasins shoes all the time stating they were comfortable. He returned once after training to find Jim Dobbin and John MacDonald had put screwing studs in them and painted on three stripes. He wasn't happy.

No one escaped the pranks. At the time, I was waiting on a new car but driving an old car that my father in law had sold me for pennies. I noticed the number plate could be worth a few quid so were looking to make a few quid from it. The lads noticed I was driving a bit of a banger so one day after training I went outside the ground and there it was, all painted up and covered in stripes with police cones covering the roof. It took me ages to get the paint off but I didn't mind as I had the last laugh. I sold the number plate for £1,000 and the traded the car for the same amount.

Eventually Allan Clarke left the club. I was devastated when he left, as he had given me the opportunity twice in my career to play for his teams. I also know that although I was playing really well, a new manager comes in with new ideas, bringing some of his old players and sometimes he doesn't fancy you. Allan Clarke was a tremendous manager and a huge influence on my career. It was a tragedy for football that he eventually drifted out of the game for good.

I know he has continued to be involved with TV work and does a lot of behind the scenes work for Leeds United, but he has been a wasted talent to football. He played for Leeds United, one of the most powerful dynasties of its era and had all the experience and knowledge from that time that could still be used to inspire young footballers. Just his stories of Leeds United could keep you listening to him for hours.

The new manager was Mel Machin, who had managed Manchester City. Within three games of his arrival, I was out. Although I didn't know it at the time, my Last game for Barnsley was against West Ham United away on New Year's Day, 1990. We lost 4–2 in an entertaining match. The following Monday morning I entered the changing rooms for the day's training. I went to my usual spot in the room, and I saw this big lad getting change using my peg. He looked at me and I looked at him. I asked him what was going on. The big lad said 'Sorry but you better go and see the gaffer'. I replied 'Don't worry, I will' and off I marched.

I banged on the manager's office door and went in. Machin asked me to sit down before telling me that the big lad was Gerry Taggart who he had bought from Manchester City and that I had been sold to Plymouth Argyle. I was dumbfounded. I told him that

I had just signed a new contract and wasn't going anywhere. He replied that I had no choice but to go because he had already spent my transfer money on Taggart and made a profit of £10,000. I still said no chance, telling him that I loved it at Barnsley. Machin quickly realised he had a problem. He told me to wait in his office and scampered off. He returned quickly with the club secretary and they offered to pay me a portion of my contract as a lump sum if I agreed to go. I quickly realised that I had no chance of playing for Barnsley again, so agreed to go to Plymouth to watch them play in a cup game at the weekend.

I travelled to Plymouth with Jan. We stayed in a nice hotel, watched the game and then negotiated with the manager, Ken Brown. I cannot say enough about Ken Brown. He was a wonderful person and a lovely man, so enthusiastic about football. You cannot help but want to play for him and so a contract was agreed. It was a very sad way to leave Barnsley, a club that had given me so much. I hoped the fans understood that I loved the club and was effectively forced out against my will.

My brother Chris later told me a story of exactly what my transfer meant to some fans. He was an Army Chaplain in the first Iraq war. He told me he got a tap on his tent once and there was this chap with a broad Barnsley accent wanting to talk to him. He thought that he perhaps had some trauma or wanted advice, but when this man found out that his name was Broddle and he was my brother, his main interest was letting Chris know that 'it was the worst thing that your Julian ever did was leave Barnsley for Plymouth Argyle'.

Chapter Six: Plymouth Argyle.

"Frame every so-called disaster in life with these words: In five years, will this matter?"

Plymouth was a different world from the north and what I had known up to that point. It was a beautiful, scenic area and the weather was nice. You had all the countryside and the coastal areas of Devon and then just down the road lay the beauty of Cornwall. It was very easy to be tempted to move there.

The only problem was that it was so far away from everything. Travelling back to see mine or Jan's parents was an epic journey, especially since we had just had our first baby. If we needed a break we tended to visit Jan's parents as my own parents were very elderly and probably not up for coping with a newborn at that stage of their life.

We used to drive to Liverpool in the middle of the night with the baby asleep in the back of the car with barely another car on the motorway.

The area was lovely though and the people were great. The lads at Plymouth Argyle were a great bunch. At the time having your hair in a perm was all the rage and I'm afraid to say that I joined in. My teammates and I used to all head off into town with our perms and have a night on the town in Plymouth. It was a great place to go out.

Amazingly, my first game for Plymouth Argyle was against Barnsley away on January 20th, 1990. To return to Barnsley so soon was very strange, especially walking into the ground and heading towards the away dressing room with my new colleagues and new manager. It was a good opportunity to see people and also to be thanked by the Barnsley fans for my time there. I really appreciated the kind words from everyone on that day. I walked onto the pitch at Oakwell and immediately felt weird. I had never wanted to leave. Once the sentimental feelings of no longer being at Barnsley passed, my primary concern was that I played well.

I wanted to put on a good performance and just make sure that I didn't momentarily forget where I was and pass to the lads in green rather than the more familiar red of my old Barnsley teammates! I was lucky in that first game to have a left-winger called Mark Robson playing in front of me. He was on loan from Spurs and a cracking little player and we immediately hit it off. I played well and we secured a one- one draw. Barnsley went on to get promotion back into the championship that year by winning at Wembley in the playoff final. I will always have a soft spot for the Tykes and I was happy as I watched that game at home, proud of the team and their fantastic supporters.

If I thought that playing well in my first game was a sign that I was going to have a fruitful career in Plymouth, then I was quickly brought down to earth with a crash. Within three weeks of signing, the manager who had brought me there, Ken Brown resigned. My heart sank and I thought 'here we go again.' John Gregory became player manager on an interim basis. John was a vastly experienced footballer who had played for big clubs and was a smooth, smart, confident man. He had good training techniques and full of enthusiasm and keen to do well. I liked him and I think if he had been given time, I think he would have done well. However, for some strange reason, the directors of Plymouth Argyle decided to overlook John and give the job to David Kemp. Kemp was from Wimbledon and believed in the traditional Wimbledon way at the time, getting the ball as fast as possible into the last third. It was far removed from the passing football that Ken Brown had advocated.

I knew I was in trouble at my first training session when Kemp told me to hit the ball forward as soon as I got it. No passing it to a colleague, no heading up the wing with the ball at my feet. Just punt it long towards the opposition box. Kemp quickly realised I wasn't that sort of player and I was told I could leave. Three weeks of feeling relatively happy at a new club and, once again, I was out the door. Kemp just wanted his players from Wimbledon and that way to play for him. Plymouth had paid good money for me, and I had committed my future to them but now I was no longer required. I didn't understand why a decent football club would move from a passing team trying to play football the right way to the Wimbledon style of play.

My main memory of my time at Plymouth will always remain the birth of our first child. He was born at Freedom Fields Hospital on Friday 13th April 1990. We loved every minute of those first few months with our new baby. I recall an away match at Newcastle around the time he was due to be born. It was the worst possible fixture being so far away from Plymouth.

I played in front of thousands of Geordie fans with a pager in my sock. I knew that if it had beeped it would mean that Jan had gone into labour and I would have walked straight off the pitch and got a flight back to Plymouth. Thankfully it wasn't required and I could see out the game. In those days teams didn't fly to away games like that, we travelled by coach. Our coach was called the 'Green Slug'.

It was a lovely green and white coach, which made its way up and down the country to away games far and wide. We spent many happy hours on the slug having a laugh and playing cards. There were always two card schools in operation. The main one was for big money, sometimes hundreds of pounds whilst the second one was for far smaller sums. Unlike some other footballers, I was never much of a gambler so I stuck to the second division level and played for pennies.

Another memory from my short time in Plymouth was meeting Heavyweight boxer Lennox Lewis. At the time, he was an up and coming boxer based in London and a teammate of mine, David 'Budgie' Byrne was mates with his promoter Frank Maloney. Budge was cocky boy but very generous, and he kindly put me up in Plymouth when I first moved there, until we found a house. He asked if I fancied going for something to eat at St Mellion Golf Club to meet Frank and Lenox. I said yes and off we went. It was a very pleasant afternoon although we were surrounded by several huge black guys sat chewing on toothpicks while we ate and chatted. I assume they were gym partners and bodyguards. The idea at the time was for Lennox to get out of the pressure of the 'big smoke' and come down to Devon to train there. It worked as he would later become the Heavyweight champion of the World.

Circumstance had meant that I was no longer wanted at Plymouth and, once again, I was left looking for a new club. In my time at Plymouth I had got to the point where I was happy that I was still in the game and playing at a reasonably high level. I still wanted that one big move, that one chance of signing for a big team to see if I could do it. I thought if I had one season where I could play well and maybe somebody would take a chance on me or one of my former managers moved to a top-flight club, but it never happened. I just wanted to be loved and wanted to be appreciated. I wanted that arm around my shoulder telling me that I was a great player. That wasn't going to happen at Plymouth so I had to leave.

I needed to find a club and a manager that wanted me. That was always a powerful attraction. If I knew someone wanted me than I was always inclined to move there. I only ever turned one club down in my career and that was Crewe Alexandra when I was playing at Barnsley. Their manager at the time was Dario Gradi and I knew he wanted me. I went to talk to him on the same day that David Platt was moving to Aston Villa. So, Platt was on his way out and I was supposedly on my way in.

The deal fell through over a plot of land. The Crewe Chairman at the time was a multi-millionaire and he owned half of Cheshire so I asked for a plot of land. He offered me a car but I wanted the plot of land. Everyone was buying plots of land in those days and you could make good money on it, so that was my focus. He refused so I decided to stick it out at Barnsley.

Now I needed to find someone who wanted me. It turned out that St Mirren would be that club and I was on my way to Scotland.

Chapter Seven: St Mirren

"When you have done something wrong, admit it and be sorry. No one in history has ever choked to death from swallowing their pride"

My move to Scotland came from nowhere. John Gregory had left Plymouth Argyle and become a football agent and asked me if he could represent me. I needed to get away from Plymouth so I immediately said yes. I had loved living in the south west but I knew I wasn't going to get a game and every footballer, even the multi-millionaires of today, will tell you that it is all about playing. If you aren't getting a game in the first team on a Saturday then you're never happy.

John Gregory was friends with another ex-player from Scotland called Gordon Smith who had played for Brighton and Glasgow Rangers. Gordon Smith was assistant manager at St Mirren and was looking for a left midfield type player. My name must have come up in conversation. Jan and I drove up to Scotland. I had no idea that the club was in Paisley. I dropped Jan off in Glasgow and got a taxi to the ground which I thought was just in another part of Glasgow.

I asked the Glaswegian taxi driver to take me to St Mirren FC and he immediately went into a rant.

"Don't you talk to me about them by the way, the Catholic bastards! They are the scum of the earth.' Apparently, the Paisley club had played Rangers that weekend and got a result against them. Clearly, the Taxi driver was a Rangers fan, and wasn't happy. 'Welcome to Scotland I thought!'

I met John Gregory at Love Street and we headed to the players' lounge. John went off to do the deal I was left looking at the pictures of St Mirren's history on the walls. He returned about one hour later and said the deal had been done and I signed, not knowing exactly what I had signed, however, I trusted John and we shook hands and he left. I never needed an agent after that, as the money wasn't big enough, so that was that last time I ever spoke to John.

I was joining the Scottish Premier League and I knew it was the top flight. That was what was important to me. I had an idea that my chance at the top flight in England had probably gone, but joining the top flight in Scotland was the next best thing. I had been aware of Graeme Souness at Rangers and bringing in players like Terry Butcher, Chris Woods and Mark Walters. That was all over our media down south, so I thought 'Well, if it's good enough for them, it's good enough for me." I knew I would be playing against Rangers and Celtic and alongside some internationals and I realised I had nothing to lose.

When we arrived in Scotland, Jan, our son and I were put up in a lovely hotel in Renfrew and stayed there for six months while we waited for a new house to be built. We were in the Bridal suite and the club had agreed to pay the bills. I loved it at the

hotel, not having to worry about food, bills or cleaning. The club even paid for friends or family to stay in a room opposite when they came to visit so being honest, I wasn't in a great hurry for our house to be finished.

My first day training I will never forget. The manager was Tony Fitzpatrick. Tony was a wonderful man in every way and he was very loyal, passionate and committed to the club. I walked onto the training field, which was right next to Glasgow airport. So much so, that when the planes came in to land, you felt you could kick a ball and almost hit the underside of them. I looked at the manager and he had two coloured bibs either side of him. He looked right at me, and said 'Which side are you on?' I replied, 'Any gaffer, totally up to you.' The gaffer repeated, 'No, which side are you on?' 'Any gaffer' I replied. He then finally asked 'Are you Protestant or Catholic?'

Religion had never been part of my football life and I never even contemplated it would ever be part of football. But this was the west of Scotland and things were different here. I told him that if anything I was Church of England so he passed me a blue bib and said 'You're on that side then'. To this day I'm still not sure how serious it was, or whether it was just a bit of banter to welcome me to Scotland. A lot of the Scottish lads in the team seemed to have a preference for one or other of the Old Firm teams and the stick would fly around the dressing room between them.

My debut game for the first team was unforgettable, except for an astonishing incident at the break. We were losing at home and not playing particularly well when halftime came. I am playing my first game for my new team, and although giving my all, I was average at best. Most of my teammates were just as poor. I get into the changing room and sit down, expecting we'll get a grilling from the boss. The manager comes in and the discussion starts.

As I am new, I keep quiet and just try to take it all in. Then, the boss turned his attention to our centre half, Roddy Manley. Words were exchanged and to my amazement, the manager dives at Roddy and a fight breaks out. Gordon Smith and others jump in quickly and split them up. I am sitting there thinking 'Have I just seen that or is this a dream?' I have never seen anything like this in my life and I'm wondering whether it was the norm in Scottish football. It was pure madness.

Strangely, it is the manager who is dragged out of the dressing room. I thought it would have been the other way around with the player being told that he would never play for the club again. Nothing more is said about the incident and we go out to play the second half. To be fair to the manager, he came in afterwards and said 'look I was out of order, it was a one-off, I shouldn't have carried on in that way.' It was totally out of character for Tony Fitzpatrick and it was never repeated. I met him last season when Raith Rovers played St Mirren and I was a guest up at Stark's Park in Kirkcaldy. It was great talking to him and catching up on old times, although I didn't bring up that particular incident.

My first game away was against Hibernian in Edinburgh. As we almost reached the ground, our keeper, Campbell Money turned to me and said, 'You're going to get pelters with a name like that. You are English and with a name like that, you've no chance'. Fortunately, it never happened. I was never really aware of getting much abuse from fans. You were aware of the big crowds and the wall of sound at Rangers or Celtic but you never really heard anything personal.

The only time I ever remember getting direct abuse was a game earlier in my career at Swindon Town. They used to shout dogs abuse and they were having a go at the fact that I was called Julian and telling me it was a girly name. Allan Clarke took me aside and said 'They are only having a go at you son because you're a good player. If you weren't a good player they would be ignoring you.' So, I took it as a compliment and it never really bothered me after that.

The first season at the club, was struggle. We had some great players but they were all individuals and not a team. We just couldn't gel. We had some cracking, talented footballers but we just couldn't do it. We were great socially. We would probably have been top of the Premier League for going out and drinking, but on the pitch, it just wasn't happening.

The team spirit was fantastic though. I developed a strong friendship with Alan Irvine, who I consider a great friend to this day. We still keep in touch and although we rarely see each other these days, when we do, it is as if I saw him yesterday. Alan was a striker at the club and had previously played for Falkirk, Liverpool, Dundee United, Shrewsbury and Mazda in Japan. Alan could drink for Scotland. He had some fantastic stories about his time in Liverpool. Kenny Dalglish had signed him for the famous club but he was mainly in the squad but not getting in the team, or at best, making the substitutes' bench. He would tell me how he would go out with all the Liverpool players socially. They were probably the best team around at the time and it is incredible to think of Alan going on the lash with the likes of Ian Rush and Jan Molby. What a character.

When we stayed over in hotels, the night before a game, Al was my roommate. Al always took a screwdriver with him on these trips and sometimes, for a laugh, we would change all the room numbers around to confuse the rest of the lads. We also would change the orders for breakfast placed outside hanging from the room doors on a card. We thought it was funny to get dry toast and a bowl of prunes delivered at 4am to the room of a team mate. It kept us amused anyway.

We once played Celtic in a cup game that was being shown on Sky. Sky TV. The broadcaster had just taken an interest in football although it was still a far cry from the wall to wall coverage and money they bring to the game today. The club did make a decent sum from the tie and handed us approximately £11,000 from the proceeds from the game. The lads decided to go to Ibiza for a week, even taking the young trainees at the club.

We made the trip to Ibiza and it was a week of pure indulgence. The weather was hot and the drinks flowed. I was staying in the same room as Al and a lad called Paul McIntyre, who was a very funny guy. As you can imagine, there was no chance of sleep, because if you did, eyebrows and other body parts would have been shaved or worse. I think I had only a few hours' sleep across the whole seven days. The majority of the squad were there for a good time, but the biggest drinkers were Al, Mark McWalter and I. We were drinking almost 24/7 and stayed in the same clothes almost for the entire week. Not a pretty sight.

Some of the younger lads had rented some mopeds and were riding them around the main square. This also happened to be where the rest of the squad were sat drinking. Al decided to jump on the back of one of the bikes and the momentum of his leap sent the moped crashing to the ground. The boys had quite nasty cuts, bruises and grazes but the rest of the squad couldn't stop laughing. After that day, they were banned from hiring mopeds by the Spanish!

Icelander Guni Torfason had issues with his passport so arrived a day late. When he got to the hotel late on that night, for some reason he couldn't get in his room. He was so frustrated he just smashed the door in. Rumour has it that he got whacked a few times by the local cops before being told to pay for the damage. It was a crazy trip and when we were flying back, I am sure I had the shakes from lack of sleep and the alcohol. If the club had been fully aware of what went on during that trip, they may have been less willing to hand us some of the cash from the Celtic game.

The drinking culture wasn't just restricted to holidays away. There were frequent nights out in Glasgow too. During the time, I was staying in the Hotel, it came to light that the lads were going into Glasgow to pubs and clubs and then coming back to my Hotel to carrying on drinking. They were cheekily charging drinks to my room account and I was brought in by the accountant and wanted to know what was going on. Before I could answer, Tony Fitzpatrick came in and had a right go at the accountant. He told him never to question me again and just to get the bill paid.

We were struggling on the field and the manager decided to go for broke by bringing in Steve Archibald and Victor Munoz from Espanyol in Barcelona. They were on huge money, which later came to light and infuriated the fans, especially as performances didn't improve.

Stevie Archibald was a former Scottish international and so aloof and such an individual that he trained on his own and did what he wanted. Stevie would go off and do his own thing. He was difficult to get to know, although eventually I gained his trust and we got on reasonably well. Victor Munoz had previously the Spanish captain and had earned sixty caps playing for his country.

Victor was always trying to make us play a different way and telling us what to do. I think most of the lads thought 'OK. We respect what you and what you've done but you aren't my manager!' Those two spent most of their time talking to each other in Spanish. I can look back at that squad now and be proud that I was playing with brilliant players. Just a shame we couldn't get it right as a team.

To make matters worse, Tony Fitzpatrick left the club and was replaced by the Celtic legend, Davie Hay. Hay brought with him some Celtic lads and I was told that if I could find a club, then he wouldn't get in the way. I felt devastated. I had come up to Scotland and tried my best and felt I had settled in to a degree. And once again I wasn't wanted. I thought 'Here we go again and where am I going to go after this?' Hay then brought a lad called David Elliot, who was a lovely lad and a super-fast left winger and so I couldn't see me getting back in the team.

Luckily for me, there were a few injuries and I was eventually given a place against Dunfermline away. I had a brilliant game and we hammered them. I even managed to score. I was being interviewed by various radio and newspapers after the game and was being asked about my transfer request. I had put in a transfer request due to not getting a game and the fact that Davie Hay didn't seem to rate me. I told the press that it still stood as I was probably just filling in until the injured lads got fit. Just a few feet away, Davie Hay was also being interviewed and was telling the press what a game I had played and that he needed to talk to me about my request.

On the Monday training after the game I was told to go to the changing rooms and wait for the manager. The boss came in and we spoke about the Dunfermline game and how well it had gone. Davie

Hay then stood in front of twenty players and apologised to me about way he had treated me.

He admitted that he'd got it wrong about me. I was shocked at the apology and when driving home I realised how much balls it must have taken for Davie Hay to say he was wrong about me in front of all of his players. For someone to show that much humility and be able to do that was impressive. From that moment on my view of him changed completely. I went home and told my wife, and in the weeks after my game was probably the best I ever played at the top level for any club. I had what I needed; confidence and a manager that believed in me.

Every week from then on, I could do nothing wrong. It was just at the start of statistics being used to analyse performance and every week my numbers were superb. Passing, running, heading, every part of my game was being rated as one of the highest in the squad. Davie Hay said to me on the training field, 'I am not sure what you have done to play the way you are, but keep doing it'. I was sky high in confidence and I didn't care who we played. I remember playing Hearts when Joe Jordan was their manager. I felt I could beat anybody. I was in that tight corner at Tynecastle with two players on me and I did the Johann Cruyff turn, beat both of them and fired in a bullet of a cross into the box. That confidence is so rare, but when you felt it, then it was a fantastic feeling. I was told at the time that

Celtic and other clubs were keeping a close watch on me.

Things off the field were good too. On June 9th 1992, at Paisley Hospital, my beautiful baby girl was born. Although we were hundreds of miles from our families, Jan's parents would meet us at the service station near Carlisle on the M6 every few weeks and take the kids for a few days. It gave us much needed space and time to recharge the batteries. It also gave Jean and Robbie time with their grandchildren. They were brilliant with our kids and helping us in any way they could and I could not have better in-laws. They were Scousers through and through and extremely proud of it and I cannot thank them enough for the help and guidance they gave us during that time.

I may have been buzzing but the team as a whole was still struggling. We had some quality players but they still weren't working as a unit. We had real talent like Chic Charnley and Thomas Stickroth. Chic was just mental. He was a cracking player but he was just hyper. He reminded me a lot of Gazza. Thomas Stickroth was the George Michael of the team. He loved himself and spent more time pruning himself in the mirror than anyone I've ever known. He was a great player though and showed moments of great talent as a winger. He was probably too much of an individual and liked to do the flashy stuff rather than picking out a teammate, but the fans loved him.

Thomas and the other foreign players used to hang around together and sometimes speak in German so that no one else could understand them. It got them into trouble once as they were in the showers criticising the manager in German. What they didn't know was that Gordon Smith had played in Austria and knew German so he heard everything they said. They never tried that again.

We also had Paul Lambert in the squad. Paul was a quiet lad and everyone called him 'Vince'. I'm not sure why. I knew he was the blue-eyed boy and had great potential but he was still young and struggling a bit with us at the time. You saw glimpses of what he was capable of and he was a cracking professional. He worked extra hard in training and he wasn't a drinker. He was good mates with Norrie McWhirter and they tended not to get involved too much in the banter that was flying around.

In an attempt to break the run of poor performances, Davie Hay had decided to take us all away to Spain. It was a little bit embarrassing as we had just played St Johnstone at home and gotten stuffed. I had scored in that game but had picked up a bit of a strain, but still went with the team. The fact that I had an injury and spent most of the trip receiving treatment meant that I was a bit removed from the rest of the squad and safe from his wrath.

The Boss had given us rules not to be out late and back in the hotel at a certain time. This was squad full of lads who loved a drink, so that was never going to happen. There were four of us watching a game in a bar one night and the alcohol was flowing. Once the match on television had finished, we thought 'stuff this, let's carry on'. We had a great night and eventually we headed back to the hotel. It was so late that we thought we'd be able to sneak back to our rooms completely unseen.

We got out of the taxi and headed into the hotel trying to keep a low profile. Unfortunately, our plan was blown out of the water as we encountered Davie Hay, sat sternly in the lobby waiting for us to arrive. He had obviously realised that not all the squad were back so had decided to sit it out and catch us in the act. He gave us a mouthful of abuse and then sent us to our rooms like chastised schoolchildren. When we got back to Scotland we were handed a fine for breaking the curfew. It was two weeks wages at first although eventually the club relented and reduced it to only one week's wage.

The press got hold of the story and, as they like nothing more than a tale of drunken footballers, so they went to town. The story wasn't helped by the fact that we were struggling in the Premier at the time and had just been hammered by St Johnstone.

We were in a relegation dogfight with Dunfermline and looking for any advantage to help us survive. Davie Hay decided to try something new and brought in a positive thinking guru called Jack Black. The theory was that he would banish all our negative thinking and make us believe in ourselves again.

The importance of the mind and positive thinking is now widely accepted in football, but at the time it was difficult to take seriously. He had us closing our eyes and thinking of positive things, like concentrating on the corner or free kick you were about to take and imaging it reaching its destination perfectly. He would also talk us through a scenario about walking towards a large mansion via a beautiful garden and flowing river. We all had our eyes closed but you can imagine lads like Chic Charnley and Alan Irvine sat there laughing and taking the piss.

The oddest exercise he had us do was to pretend there was a dry shower in the dressing room. We eventually had some streamers put up, hanging from the ceiling to simulate the shower. We were supposed to stand under the shower before training and before games to wash off any doubts in our mind or negative thoughts.

It was all new and a bit too much for most lads at that time. Most did it for a while and then it was quickly forgotten. One player who did seem to take it on board more than most was Paul Lambert. He was very positive about it and I think he used it in his own way for many years afterwards. Paul went on to have an incredibly successful career playing for Celtic and went on to win the Champions League with Borussia Dortmund, so maybe there was something in it after all.

Eventually the failure to bond on the field caught up with us and we were relegated to the second tier of Scottish football. The end of season trip away was slightly surreal that year as we were in a resort with the Dunfermline and Sunderland squads, and we quickly realised that all three teams had been relegated that season. It was a strange situation as there was nothing to celebrate for any of us, but that didn't stop us making the most of it every night.

If life in the Scottish First Division was going to be tough, then it was made tougher by the fact that Davie Hay left the club. His replacement was Jimmy Bone, a man who had made 131 appearances for St Mirren a player and had previously been managing Power Dynamos in Zambia. Straight away, my days were numbered at the club.

Although we had been relegated, I personally had just had one of my best seasons for a long time. I had won numerous awards from different sponsors and supporters clubs that season and assumed that my place in the team was secure. Jimmy Bone clearly had other ideas. I will never know why the new manager took a dislike to me, but from day one, it was made clear that I would be better looking for another club. I felt even before I had kicked a ball for him, that I was no longer required. Bone reminded me a lot of Mick Buxton at Scunthorpe.

They put the focus on aggression and young lads that would do anything they asked. Perhaps they didn't think that I would run through a brick wall for them, that my style of play wasn't direct enough or I would cause problems for them. Regardless, I wasn't in their long-term plans.

The season started and a long list of injuries in the squad meant I was drafted into the first team to start against Raith Rovers. I was carrying an injury myself at the time, but the team were so desperate that I ended up taking to the field at Stark's Park. The Raith Rovers manager at the time was Jimmy Nicholl, the ex-Manchester United and Northern Ireland defender. His assistant was a familiar face from my Plymouth days, Martin Harvey. Martin had been there at the beginning when Ken Brown had signed me for Plymouth. They had assembled a good squad of talented lads but we were the newly

relegated team and favourites for the title. This game was supposed to be the start of our comeback, which would ultimately end in promotion back to the Premier League. How wrong we were.

From the moment we kicked off, Raith Rovers just blew us away. Players like Peter Hetherston, Gordon Dalziel and Craig Brewster just destroyed us with crisp passing football and deadly finishing and by the final whistle we trudged back towards the dressing room having lost 7-0. It was the biggest defeat of my career and as the famous saying goes, we were lucky to get the nil. I will never know to this day how we played so badly, but perhaps the reality was that it was just that Raith Rovers played really well. This was to be the start of a golden period in the history of the Kirkcaldy club and the Rovers fans still fondly recall that match as the one that kick started it all.

It is strange to think that after such an embarrassing defeat that I would later sign for Rovers. I can only assume that Jimmy Nicholl and Martin Harvey saw something in me that day despite the horrendous performance and embarrassing score line. It remains a painful memory and was a match that I was never allowed to forget by the lads and management when I did eventually join the Stark's Park dressing room.

That match set the tone for the season. We never got going as a team and never really troubled the promotion battle. Raith Rovers ran away with the title and a strong Kilmarnock side joined them in promotion to the Premier League. I continued to struggle under the management of Jimmy Bone, with first team appearances limited.

Towards the end of the season, I got a call from Scunthorpe United and I went back there for a month's loan, playing six games for my old club. I was just delighted to be away from Paisley and to have an opportunity to play at their new stadium, which I'd just missed out on when transferred to Barnsley.

Bill Green was now the manager and it was nice to be wanted. I had been struggling at St Mirren and I wasn't really fit enough, but the month was a reasonable success, although I'm sure the Scunthorpe fans remembered me being slightly quicker in my younger days! One of my six games in September 1992 was against a Leeds United team containing Eric Cantona and Gary Speed, so it was a privilege to be able to share the field alongside two football giants.

With the season over it was time to leave St Mirren. Despite all the ups and downs, I had really enjoyed my time at the Paisley Club. I was leaving a fantastic bunch of players and with some great friends and brilliant memories. During the Davie Hay era, I felt I was at the top of my game and playing to the maximum of my ability.

That was a rare feeling throughout my career, so it was a special time. By the time I left, my confidence had been shattered. I had become a very average player and was relying on work rate alone to get me through games. Looking back, a lot of the change I attribute to the management style of Jimmy Bone.

It felt like he had effectively destroyed me and my confidence. His training, his aggressive and angry attitude and how he treated the players. It was exactly the opposite of what I needed and my game suffered badly as a result. By the end of my time at St Mirren, I had gone from one of the better players in the squad scoring regularly, to not being able to hit a barn door.

When Bone told me that Partick Thistle were interested in me, I jumped at the chance to move. They were still in the Premier League and based in Glasgow, so I wouldn't have to move from Erskine and could start afresh at a new club with a new manager who hopefully rated me. I was sad to leave Paisley, as I'd had some great times there, but it was time for another new challenge.

Chapter Eight: Partick Thistle

"Doubt kills more dreams than failure ever will"

I only played five times for Partick Thistle, and I will be the first to admit that I didn't do myself justice in my time at the Glasgow club. My confidence was at an all-time low after my experience with Jimmy Bone and I was very poor. It wasn't a great point in my career.

It was a vicious cycle. You play poorly and then get so angry and frustrated with yourself for not playing so well. Then you put more and more pressure on yourself and the stress starts to kick in. You think 'Why can't I just do one good pass and get a cheer?' It goes from bad to worse and you don't know how to get out of it. You are waiting for something to happen to turn it around. I felt I just needed that one good game where it clicked but it never happened at Partick Thistle.

I was never there long enough and I felt like I was letting the lads down. You then start to get that feeling in your head that all the lads are talking about you and asking the question 'Why has he signed him? He's shit.' All I was doing was running up and down the wing and making the odd pass.

We had a great bunch of lads and a very eccentric manager in John Lambie. He had very unusual training methods to say the least. The first challenge would be finding somewhere to train. We would frequently be driving through Glasgow, looking for a spare bit of land and we would invariably end up on a gravel pitch, often with dogs running around and once with a tramp living in a homemade tent not far from where we were practising.

Once we started training, Lambie would often leave it to others to take the sessions. He would be off to the side on his own practising his golf swing. He would often chip golf balls over our heads as we trained. Thankfully he was good enough to make sure that none of the lads ever got hit.

Sometimes we wouldn't even see a football from one Saturday to the next. We would do gym work or running up and down the stands or we would head to a local gym and just swim or do the steam rooms. When some of the lads raised the fact that we weren't actually playing football with the manager, he just replied, 'If you don't see a football for a week, then when Saturday comes, you will all be hungry to get the ball and not give it away!' I'm not sure it was a theory that was ever proved correct on a match day.

Lambie wrote in one of the first programmes when he obtained my services that I had a wonderful left foot and given time, will be a great asset to the club. He stated 'He has the best left foot in the Premier

League'. In the end, it only sought to heap more pressure on me and regrettably I never lived up to his impressive billing. I tried to compensate with hard work but it got to the point that I didn't want the ball, and when I did get it, I only had one thing in mind, which was to quickly get rid of it and pass the ball on. I was player who was meant to take players on and then get past them and put a cross over. But my confidence was shot and I wasn't sure how to get it back.

After a few weeks, I had a chat with the manager about my confidence. We both knew that something wasn't quite right. It was suggested that I see a hypnotist to get me back on track. I went to see this male hypnotist in Glasgow. He asked me to lie on the treatment table and close my eyes. I wasn't entirely convinced but did as he said and off he went. It was similar to the Jack Black thinking I had experienced at St Mirren, focusing on keeping positive and believing in my abilities.

The sessions were recorded and I did used to listen to them before games. Reflecting back on it now, I don't think at that stage of life I was fully in touch with my feminine side so perhaps I didn't engage with it as effectively as I could. I think with hindsight it may have worked if I'd have been more open-minded but I was still reasonably young at the time.

Thistle was a struggling team, just above the bottom three, but had some decent players. We had the likes of Craig Nelson, Paul McLaughlin, Ian

Cameron, Albert Craig, Gerry Britton, Davie Irons, George Shaw and Isaac English. They were all great lads and doing the best they could, but it was difficult when you were up against the likes of Rangers and Celtic. I remember once getting a hard-working draw away against Celtic, but you frequently came away with nothing from hostile grounds like Celtic Park and Ibrox Stadium.

I played so rarely that I don't remember many of the games. One that does stick out was a home game against Dundee United in February 1993. United were fairly high up in the league standings and we were third bottom. Duncan Ferguson was playing for Dundee United and causing us all sorts of problems. He was a tall gangly forward that was great in the air and had a lot of ability on the ground.

Just before half-time, he scored a goal and turned away celebrating with his colleagues and we all started to make our way back towards the centre circle to prepare for the re-start. If I remember correctly, one of our players even picked up the ball and threw it to our keeper to kick downfield towards the centre spot.

To everyone's astonishment the referee waved his arms high up and basically said play on! There was immediate confusion, but this quickly turned to joy for us as we realised that a legitimate goal had just been ruled out. You could imagine the protests from the Dundee United players all running towards the referee demanding him to re-instate the goal.

I think everybody in the ground including the seagulls sat on the stadium roof saw the goal had seen the ball cross the line and rebound off the stanchion, but the referee and his assistant hadn't and that was all that mattered. Thankfully there was no goal line technology back then. Within a minute, he blew for halftime and we walked off the pitch trailing 2-0 but grateful for the non-goal that should have been awarded. The referee was harassed all the way down the Firhill tunnel by Dundee United players, management and backroom staff. In the end, it didn't make any difference to the result as United went on to hammer us 4-0. The season continued and Thistle stayed up. We may not have had any superstars but they were honest, hard-working professionals who did their best to keep Thistle in the Premier league. It was a remarkable achievement. John Lambie was a wonderful man, a little eccentric for sure, but he loved the club and was their heartbeat in that era. He gave me a chance and it is a regret that I didn't give him the true me on the field. My confidence was shot through. I was hopeless and didn't deserve to be in that team.

That summer I was approached by Raith Rovers and decided to leave Firhill and try my luck at a new club. My only hope was that I could regain my confidence and some of the form I had shown earlier in my football journey. At the time, I wasn't aware then that it was to be the defining move of my football career.

Chapter Nine: Raith Rovers

"Success is not final, failure is not fatal. It is courage to continue that counts"

I arrived at Raith Rovers not knowing what lay ahead. I was still recovering from experience at Partick Thistle and wasn't sure if I could regain my best form. Time would tell, but I was just pleased that someone had shown some faith in me and given

me the opportunity. I think the decision to sign me had been heavily influenced by Martin Harvey, who was

an assistant to Jimmy Nicholl and who had been at Plymouth Argyle when I had joined the south west club. 'Harv' had vast experience of the game, and after all the years in the game, still had the same enthusiasm as if he was just starting out in football. I think they wanted another squad player with experience of playing at a certain level to do a job for them. I got the nod to go and speak to Jimmy Nicholl. I was immediately struck by his enthusiasm for the game. He had seen it all in a tremendous playing career. He had played for Manchester United, Sunderland, West Bromwich Albion, Glasgow Rangers and Rover's big rivals Dunfermline. He had also featured in two World Cups for Northern Ireland so his experience was unquestionable. He was player manager and was still young enough to turn out for the first team when required. He had that Irish charm and wit about him, and he was the sort of person you could never have an argument with, as you respected him too much. He was definitely one of the good guys in football, a good all-round family man with strong morals who was unscrupulously fair.

He had taken Raith Rovers, a relatively small club with modest finances into the Scottish Premier League for the first time and assembled a squad of talented footballers that could play a bit. I was aware of just how good the team was, having been stuffed 7-0 by them in my time at St Mirren. They had gone on to win the league comfortably that season and I thought maybe with that quality of player around about me and with Martin Harvey in my corner, I might turn myself around and have a good couple of years here.

We chatted and Jimmy offered me a two-year contract. He was very enthusiastic and clearly wanted me, and I was happy to commit myself to the club. Part of the deal was the club allowing me to rent a lovely property in a place called Dalgety Bay, which is fantastic area to live, with magnificent views of the Forth Bridges and the Edinburgh silhouette in the distance. We rented for around six months until I sold my house in Erskine and could buy a new home in Fife.

Raith Rovers were now in the Premier League and looking to consolidate. They wanted experience and a bigger squad in case of injuries and to provide competition. Jimmy Nichol had persuaded the club Chairman and his board to support full-time football. This meant a few of their players had left as they couldn't take the risk with their full-time jobs. When I arrived, it was a mixture of free transfers like myself, older experienced players, and young kids brought through the youth system or acquired from junior teams.

The first few days training was a shock to the system, having just left Thistle where you could never be sure if there was going to be any training facilities from one day to the next. Rovers trained on the same local park every day and the training was well organised and thorough. It was fun but it was hard work. My confidence was low and watching these lads train and play football, I knew how tough it was going to be to get in this team. I also had that new boy feeling and was initially concentrating on

trying to fit in. In the first few weeks at a new club you really wanted to get involved but you tend to talk when spoken to and it can feel like you are on the edge of everything. Thankfully at Raith Rovers the characters in the dressing room had no such reluctance to get me involved. When I walked into the changing rooms for the very first time, the abuse and piss-taking began immediately. When you have people like Gordon Dalziel, Peter Hetherston and Jock McStay as teammates then there was no hiding place. Nobody got immunity from the stick they gave out, not even the new boy.

The team was packed with talent. Peter Hetherston was the captain and ran the show on and off the field. He was almost like an assistant manager at times, even calling the gaffer Jimmy. Raith Rovers had given Peter a new lease of life and his performances in centre midfield showed. He played with no stress and, at times, looked a world-beater.

Our keeper at Raith Rovers was Scott Thomson. Thommo became my roommate on away days. He kept a tidy room and would always be available to make a nice brew for me on trips away! I could always rely on him for entertainment as he would bring a golf game for us and we passed many an hour pre-match playing electronic golf. As a 'keeper was steady as a rock and I cannot remember him ever letting us down, although he might say he did when he got sent off during our League Cup run, although that turned out not too bad in the end. He was solid, reliable, agile and dominating in his area. He was a very grounded and a good family man. He was very supportive to me and gave much-needed pep talks when I wasn't in the team or thought I might get dropped. I will always consider him as a good friend.

At the back were Shaun Dennis, and Davie Sinclair. They were two tough tackling, no holding back centre halves, who would tell you in the game if you were not doing enough.

117

Shaun Dennis would have run through a brick wall for the club. He could play a bit, but also, took no prisoners. He was tough, strong and good in the air and nobody would get past him. He was very intimidating to look at and very aggressive in a match, but strangely, was relatively quiet on the field. He was never an over the top shouter and said what he had to when he had to, and no more. When you played alongside him, you knew you could rely on him 100%.

Sinky was a no holds, straight talking, tough tackling player. What you see is what you got with him. He would kick his own grandmother if he thought it would secure the club three points. Most of the time, he played centre half, but would move into midfield when required. Whatever the manager said, Sinky totally believed in it and gave his all for every ninety minutes. He may not have been the most accomplished footballer skill wise, but he did the job and had a never say die attitude. I had the odd heated exchange with Sinky in the middle of a match, but I knew it was only because of his passion to win. He was Mr Raith Rovers and epitomised the underdog spirit of the club at the time.

At right back during my time in Kirkcaldy, there were three possible contenders. The first was John 'Jock' McStay. Jock was coming to the end of his Raith Rovers career when I arrived but he was very popular amongst the lads and with the fans. He was very reliable and did everything simply but effectively on the pitch, a good player that never let you down. He was also a prankster with the other Glasgow lads that travelled together in one car.

Unfortunately, he will always be remembered for the assault by Duncan Ferguson in a match at Ibrox which landed the Rangers striker in jail. Big Dunc head-butted John and there was an investigation later which, combined with previous offences, led to him serving at her majesty's pleasure.

Poor John took a lot of stick from Rangers fans for years after the incident and this might have had an influence on him not getting another contract with the club. The story was that the directors at the time may have thought it was bad publicity for the club.

Another option at right back was Jason Rowbotham. Jason was Welsh and played at Plymouth Argyle when I was there and I think he had only been let go due to a few injuries he had in that time. He was steady and reliable with strong tackling and could ping a great ball. He had a good engine and I never saw him struggle on any hard training session. I think I can honestly say that whenever Jason played in the first team, he never put a foot wrong. Jimmy Nichol knew that Jason would never let him down and could put him in various positions when required. The problem for me was that he was so consistent and so versatile that he was also a major threat to my position throughout my Raith Rovers career.

Jason was also a bit of a joker, and good for the team morale. He was another of the bunch of lads that you could find on the golf course, or out in town for a night out.

He was always up to something, usually playing a practical joke on somebody. We developed a mutual respect for each other, but I think we always knew that we were rivals for a place the first team, and I feel if it wasn't for that, we might have been a lot closer as mates.

The last right back was Steve McAnespie who was a bit of an eccentric to say the least. Steve came along to join us from playing in Sweden so although he was young, he had great experience. When he first joined the club, he came across as quiet and difficult to work out or understand. At first, I couldn't really see what Jimmy Nichol saw in him, however, as time went by, he opened up and became an integral part of the team and a very solid performer.

I guess that's why I am not a successful manager like Jimmy Nicholl! Steve went about his business on the pitch as a steady player that liked to push forward when he could. He was very fit and settled into the team as if he had always been there. He was eventually sold to Bolton Wanderers for a lot of money, which the club appreciated.

The other thing to mention about Steve was that he liked a drink. I can still see him now in my mind, sitting with a bottle of Brandy. It didn't matter to

Steve whether he had people with him or not, he was happy just drinking and talking to himself! We went to Ireland on a trip for a few days to get away and do some team bonding. On one of the mornings I headed down to breakfast with Scott Thomson. We had been out for a drink the night before but it hadn't been a late one so I was ready for some breakfast and some light training.

We entered the restaurant and bar area and there was Steve McAnespie. He was sat by himself still drinking Brandy and smashed out of his face. We knew that the manager and Martin Harvey would be down shortly so we hid the drink and got it into Steve's head that he had to act normal. Jimmy Nicholl and Martin Harvey arrive and after acknowledging the three of us, head off to sit at a different table, thankfully one some distance from us. We start to eat breakfast and after a while I turn around to see Steve asleep with his head in his bowl of cereal.

We quickly woke him up and got him up to his room out of the sight of the gaffer. To our amazement, Steve is back down for training an hour later and even though Jimmy Nicholl had decided to put us through a tough session, Steve managed to get through it. I don't think the gaffer had any idea Steve was off his face during the session!

Up front was Gordon Dalziel. Daz was one of the biggest characters at the club, once met never forgotten! He had scored goals for fun at Raith

Rovers over the years, and like any good striker, he had total belief in his ability. He was a hard worker but could moan for Scotland, if you didn't get the ball to him. Daz knew that if you got the supply of crosses to him, he would score every game. He scored nearly all his goals in the six and eighteen-yard box. He very rarely scored that spectacular goal but he didn't need to.

Daz was a very funny guy with a brilliant sense of humour. He was always looking to take the piss and if you gave a little dig at him in return then he would always come back at you with his quick wit. His practical jokes were legendary.

I remember once Daz and a few of the other lads set up Peter Hetherston in spectacular fashion. Peter was a very confident lad and I think he thought he could go on and do anything he wanted in life. So, the lads decided to send him a letter from BBC Scotland saying that they had seen him on TV and asking if he fancied a small part in a Taggart show. Taggart was a detective show set in Scotland which pulled in huge ratings at the time.

When Peter got the letter, he was beaming from ear to ear. He made a point of telling all the lads that he'd got a casting for the programme. He clearly loved the attention. When he finally got to the date to attend the studios, he went and of course, was gutted when the staff there had no idea what he was talking about. You can imagine the abuse he took at training the next day!

Alongside Daz in attack was Ally Graham. Ally was one of the lads that travelled to Kirkcaldy with the other Glasgow boys. You can imagine the banter they had in that car. The time they spent travelling together helped them all develop a close bond with each other, and I think helped the rest of the team have that special camaraderie we had during the time I was there.

Ally was a bit of a talker and always had a story for any topic mentioned. If you mentioned you had scored a goal from 20 yards, you could be sure that Ally had scored a goal from the halfway line. You took what he said with a pinch of salt but he was a lovely bloke and great company. He was a decent player too. He was a big lad, good in the air and could play a bit on the ground as well.

Raith Rovers at the time had a few young lads coming through the ranks that would go on to be part of the history of the club. They had all cost nothing and were all just getting into the team and establishing themselves.

Stevie Crawford was a striker but with pace and good attitude. He would chase any ball put in the corners and had a good engine. He would be the guy that scored the first goal in the League Coca Cola Cup and he would go on to play for Scotland. Stevie was always up to no good winding his colleagues up, especially Ronnie Coyle and some of the older lads, as he knew they couldn't match him for pace so would never catch him. I have spent many a night out with Stevie, and he was a great guy to go out with.

Jason Dair was best mates with Stevie Crawford, and if my memory serves me well, had made his debut in the match where Rovers thrashed my St Mirren team 7-0. He had even scored in that game. Jason spent most of his playing time at Raith on the wing, or just inside, and had a quality strike of the ball. Jason was fast and fit, although a little moody at times on the field, which I know he won't thank me for saying! I think out of all the younger lads that were in the first team, I think Jason was the one I didn't get to know as well as I should have, but that's not to say if I called him up now, the bond and history we shared wouldn't still be there.

Jason and Stevie seemed to be attached at the hip and they seemed to do everything together, even when we were out socialising. Jason was a very good golfer too, one of the best at the club on our famous golf days out.

One of the most loyal players at the club was Robert Raeside. Robbie was so unlucky with serious injuries, but it just wouldn't stop him having the faith to come back again and fight to get a spot in the first team squad. He was a nice lad, always positive, and a good strong centre half too. I think he was an inspiration to the rest of us, as he just kept coming back after each injury.

Sometimes it felt like Robbie should have just moved into the treatment room as it's there where he spent all of his time. He was always in there or out on pushbikes, riding along the coastal routes of the Kingdom of Fife. He would later decide to train up as a physiotherapist, so there was one silver lining for being so unlucky with injuries.

The last of the younger players was Colin Cameron. 'Mickey' was, in my opinion, the best footballer at the time of his age, in Scotland. He played midfield and just had that quality about him. He was a little smaller than the usual footballer, but what he lacked in height he made up for with speed, ability and enthusiasm. He would get up and down the field and always appeared to have enough strength to play for another ninety minutes. He would run opponents into the ground, and then use his class to press forward.

I have said before that Mickey should have played for the likes of Manchester United, but it never happened. However, he did go on to play for Hearts, Wolves and Scotland, and won a few more trophies along the way. I cannot speak highly enough about Mickey Cameron, and if it wasn't for the younger players like him, Robbie, Jason, Stevie and Sinky as a core part of the team, then I might have missed out on a wonderful time of my football career.

There a few other lads that were either part of the squad at the time, or joined as the seasons passed.

Barry Wilson joined us in 1994 but had already played a cup round for his previous club, Ross County and therefore, ineligible to play for Raith Rovers in the League Cup that year. Now I thought I was fast in my day, but Barry could have given Carl Lewis a run for his money. He was super-quick and when he put the ball past his opponent then there will be only one winner to the ball. Off the pitch, he was outgoing and very laid back. I don't think I ever saw Barry in a huff.

Danny Lennon joined us from Hibernian and would go on to replace Peter Hetherston as captain when he left the club to sign for Aberdeen. Danny was a great lad with fantastic ability. He very quickly adapted to our ways and became an integral part of the team. He played midfield and dominated the middle of the park.

He was a busy player and was great at the pass and move play, and could get from the box to box all day long. He was a super fit guy, who was one of the first that I saw trying new diets and power foods to help him to be even fitter. Danny didn't moan at all, and always a positive player on and off the field.

Davie Kirkwood joined us in late August 1994. Davie was a very experienced player having previously played for East Fife, Rangers, Hearts and then Airdrie. During the period I was there, Davie had a few injuries, and was in and out of the team. However, he got on with his job, and was a steady player. In my presence, Davie was a quiet lad, but I am sure when he was in the car with the Glasgow lot, I am sure he would have given out stick as much as taking it.

Tony Rougier joined the squad and was a strong tricky winger from Trinidad and Tobago. He had tons of ability and showed it many times. I felt there was so much more to get from him and we all knew it. I wish when at Rovers, that Tony played on my side more often as he would have been a fantastic partner on the left. It certainly would have helped me to get up and down, knowing he would cover for me if I went beyond him, but regrettably he tended to play the right wing all the time.

Tony was a typical laid-back Caribbean man, who just went with the flow and was cool with it. The only thing Tony seemed to have a problem with was swearing. He refused to swear and all the lads were always trying to get him to, but instead, Tony would make up words to replace the bad language!

Alex Taylor was another who joined Raith Rovers in the second part of my career at the club. Alex was a super fit athlete, and loved doing triathlons off-season. He could run all day and I could only dream of his fitness ability. He was another solid professional who was steady and never let you down when he played. Alex was a very intelligent, well-spoken man and was not one for being involved in the banter and set ups, but that didn't stop him being a great teammate.

The last two teammates to mention are unfortunately no longer with us, Ronnie Coyle and Ian Redford. It is with a heavy heart that I recall these two great guys who it was a privilege to play alongside.

There was not a nicer person in football at the time I played than Ronnie Coyle, although he could moan a bit, but that was because he wanted to be in the team and hated messing up in training or in a game. Ronnie was a fixture at the club having played for eight years at Raith Rovers. He was brought to the club by previous manager Frank Connor, having previously played for amongst others, Middlesbrough, Rochdale and Celtic. Ronnie Coyle was mainly a defender, but he liked to push forward into midfield when possible. If Ronnie had one weakness it was that he was very serious during a game.

I suppose some would say you have to be, but I sometimes thought being so intense, he would put himself under too much pressure in games and that resulted in the odd mistake. He was a quality player though and was one of those lads, who would help the younger lads at the club, advising and passing on his experience. Ronnie took time out to do this, and it would never be a problem for him. Ronnie travelled through from the west with the other Glasgow lads, and from what I can gather took a lot of stick from them at times. It was all good natured and he held his own.

There's a famous story of Daz having won a top of the range golf jumper at one of our golf away days. As they were driving home, he had to listen to Daz bragging about his win and telling them how good he was at golf. Ronnie asked to have a look at the jumper, then promptly opened the car window and threw it out onto the Forth Road Bridge. It was never seen again. I would love to have seen Ronnie's face knowing he had one up on Daz!

Ronnie was diagnosed with Leukaemia in 2009. It was an illness that he couldn't shake and one of the saddest days of my football life was playing at Starks Park in March 2011. I travelled up from South Yorkshire to Scotland to be part of a benefit match for Ronnie to raise awareness of the disease, knowing that my former teammate was coming to the end of his short, but wonderful life. All the guys from the 1994 cup winning team who could be there turned up. I knew why we were all coming, but I wasn't sure what I would say or do meeting Ronnie after all these years in such difficult circumstances.

Upon arrival at the club, it was wonderful to see all the old familiar faces and walking onto that park again brought back some amazing memories. I approached Ronnie just as he was being hugged by everyone, and when we looked at each other, I just saw that incredible smile on his face. It was incredibly emotional but at the back of my mind I was just thinking 'keep it together and be strong for Ronnie.' I thought 'we are here today for him, and if

Ronnie has the strength to be there and be happy, then I needed to get a grip, and be strong too'. We had a quick chat before he was whisked away by other ex-players, family or friends, as everybody wanted to have a part of Ronnie that special day. Raith Rovers veterans played Celtic veterans but the

actual game was insignificant as it was all about Ronnie. As expected, Ronnie was given a standing ovation by all supporters and players, and when he was handed the microphone to say a few words, he could not do it at first as he had so much emotion inside him. I was heartbroken as I watched the bravest man you could ever want to see walk off the pitch to allow the game to start. It is at moments like these that you realise that worrying about all the stupid stuff you worry about in life, like earning money or having the latest model of car mean very little. The game passed by, and then we all showered, and got ready as there was an evening of food and entertainment at a local hotel in Kirkcaldy. It was a fantastic night with special guest speakers.

When Ronnie said a few words, and spoke about football and his family, I was welling up. After the meal, it was down to mainly all the lads from Raith Rovers. I could tell Ronnie was feeling quite weak by the time he got his family off to their rooms.

However, he wanted to stay up and be with all the lads for one last time. The drinks flowed into the early hours, until it was time to go to bed. We got the chance to talk to him and have a last pint of beer with him, and that night is something that I will treasure for the rest of my life. It was a beautiful, but heart-breaking day and I was devastated that Ronnie passed away two weeks later at the age of just 46. It must have taken all his strength to make it through that day, but he was a fighter on and off the pitch. God bless you Ronnie Coyle.

The other teammate who we have since lost was Ian Redford. He joined Raith Rovers towards the end of his career, and came to the club to add that little bit of extra experience. Ian had started his career at Dundee, and made his debut as a substitute for them at 17 years old. He signed for Rangers in 1980, for then a Scottish record fee of £210,000 and went on to play for the Glasgow club 172 times. When he arrived at Raith, he was in the process of gaining his coaching badges with the intention of becoming a manager. During the short time I knew Ian, I considered him a very intelligent, quiet and respectful man and I enjoyed his company.

He joined Scott Thomson, David Narey and myself driving back and forth to the training pitches in Kirkcaldy. At the time, stupidly, I wasn't aware of the two legends I was sharing the car with. They were just my Rovers' teammates. Ian never mentioned his past and was just a nice humble man, who was happy to be at the club near the end of his playing career. At no time, did I ever sense that Ian had some inner demons, although he was very quiet and serious about his job. That his life would later be taken away in such tragic circumstances was incredibly sad. Rest in peace my friend.

Despite having such talented teammates, my first few months at Raith Rovers didn't start too well. My confidence was low after Partick Thistle and I was taking my usual time to settle in a new club. The team had just won promotion and looked the part in every department. When I watched people like Peter Hetherston and Mickey Cameron brimming with confidence and knocking the ball about in training, I felt I was miles away from establishing myself in the first team.

The pre-season matches were tough for me, as I felt I was trying to catch up to the others. They all had the banter of a tight knit squad at that point, I felt would take a long time to break into their group. I was going home to Jan looking down and troubled.

Jimmy Nicholl had high expectations and was obviously expecting more from me. The gaffer was not aware of my lack of confidence, and was probably, wondering if he had made a mistake signing me. After just a few weeks, I was called into his office. He sat me down and told me that he  would pay me off and give me a year of my contract to leave. To this day Jimmy swears that he didn't, but I remember it as clear as day. What a start to my Raith Rovers career! I said to him 'No chance, I'm not going anywhere' and that I would fight for my place at the club. I had no option. I knew that I had failed at Partick Thistle and that if I failed at Raith Rovers then there were, realistically, very few places for me to go after that. I then buckled down and started to try and make an impact at the club. I slowly got my chance in the first team, and it seemed I was in the team for one or two, then out of the team for a few. The club were enjoying being in the Premier League and playing at all the big grounds, but although we put in some great performances, we continued to struggle near the bottom of the league. Eventually I established myself as the left back and wing back, and never looked back.

My position as the only left sided player in the team was tough at times. The right back usually had a right-winger to help out, typically Jason Dair, Barry Wilson and eventually Tony Rougier. They sometimes came over to my side but this was rare. Most games I had to patrol up and down the left side on my own, trying to get up to support any attack and cross the ball for the front lads, then trying to get back to defend in the back four. It was a demanding shift and I would be breathing out of my backside at times. The manager clearly thought I was capable though as I eventually got that position to myself.

Although I had established myself, the season ended in relegation. Three teams were relegated out of the top flight that year due to league reconstruction and although we had a talented squad, we perhaps didn't have the same experience of playing in the top flight as other clubs around us had. We would play well and come away with nothing, whilst other sides would dig deep and come away with a victory or a draw. It was a disappointment but I was now well established in the squad and looked forward to helping the club try to bounce back. Little did I know that the following season would prove to be the defining season of my career.

I was on a social media site a few days ago, and saw the saltire flag of Scotland and written on it were the words, "JULIAN IS GOD, BRODDLE PURE GENIUS" Also on it was Raith Rovers. I was shocked and obviously amazed to see this flag after all these years, as for one, I had never seen it before, and two, who would actually take all that time to put my name on a Scottish Raith Rovers flag.

It is not the best name in the World to put on a flag and I am sure a Gordon Dalziel or Stevie Crawford written on the flag would suit far better than my name, plus they were Scottish.

The photograph of the flag had been put on by a Raith Rovers supporter called Chris Willett. He had said of the site that he had taken the flag all the way to Munich and the Cup final and it was still looking good after all these years.

I was totally blown away. I clearly had to reply to the message and said that I just cannot believe it has my name of the said flag and I also put "WOW". Another guy called Don Manson, responded by saying that I had underestimated my popularity and that I was still a hero to many Raith Rovers supporters. I was so surprised and amazed and thankful.

The fact that I wasn't Scottish and I played in the same team as some fantastic players at the club, and yet these lads and Chris Willett had decided to stick my name on their treasured flag that they took with them to such important games in the clubs' history and their history. I know a few weeks previously, that I discovered on the same social media site, some of the Raith Rovers supporters had been calling me "Scoop".

Now this again, was something new to me. I couldn't resist asking these guys, why they called me scoop and how come I had no idea about it when I played for Raith Rovers all those years ago.

A couple of the lads replied by saying it was a name I was given because I would play the long ball often down the line to the forwards and it was the way I pinged the ball. I took it as a compliment and they said that it was a compliment. Believe me, I have been given a lot worse names over the years. I knew there was a bunch of lads that stood right behind the home dugout that shouted to me every home game, but I had no idea about the name and the flag.

Again, I feel humbled by people that love their football team and appreciate the efforts that I liked to think I did while I was there. I thank you and will treasure the new memories I have from the incredible Raith Rovers supporters.

Chapter Ten: An Incredible Season

"Live in such a way that if somebody spoke badly of you, no one would believe it"

The start of season 1994-95 was much like any other. There was a hangover from relegation the previous season, but the lads were determined to bounce back and get back to the Premier League. We knew there were strong sides in our division like Dundee and local rivals Dunfermline, but we had confidence that our squad was strong and could compete.

I was established in the team and playing well, but results in the early part of the season just weren't going our way. We were waiting for something to click. It was our League Cup campaign that offered us a break from the pressure of winning promotion, and what a campaign it turned out to be.

The start of our League Cup campaign was at Ross County up in the Highlands, the club that I would later join at the end of my career. We travelled up to Dingwall on 17th August, 1994 not even thinking about reaching the final. It was just a case of get the job done against a lower league team and move on to the next round. I was a substitute for some reason, but I took it on the chin and accepted it's a squad situation and decisions like that are made from time to time.

Anyway, the first half of the match wasn't that too great to mention, and Ross County probably had the best chance. We got back into the changing rooms at half-time and Jimmy Nicholl wasn't happy how we played. He let us know just how poor we had been and how he expected more from us in the second half. The message must have got through as when the lads went back out it was a totally different game.

A wonderful hat trick from Ally Graham, one from Dazza and one from Mickey Cameron, gave us a comfortable 5 - 0 victory. It was a fantastic start to the campaign and made a life a lot easier for the long trip back to Fife. Ally Graham won £500 from the sponsors Coca Cola, but the rest of us never saw any of it. At the time, we thought it was just another cup game and I don't think anyone around the club had an incline that it would be the start to one of the most historic cup runs in Scottish football.

We had only set our sights on trying to get back to the Premier again at the first attempt, and we probably thought the cups were a bit of a distraction.

The next round we were drawn against Kilmarnock. They had been promoted with Rovers in season 1992-93 but had managed to stay up and were still a Premier League club. On the last day of August, they visited Stark's Park. This was the game that

David Narey made his debut for the club. Davie had spent his entire career with Dundee United, until his last season with us at Raith Rovers. During his illustrious career with Dundee United, he won a Scottish Premiership title and two Scottish cups, and including representing his country in a World Cup. Not only representing them, but also scoring against the wonderful team of Brazil. Davie played over 600 games for Dundee and 35 times for Scotland. Throughout his long career, it was very well known that Davie would not do interviews, and if he ever did, it would have been a brownie point for the person that got the interview. However, in the one season that I got to know Davie, he was talkative, intelligent, funny and a massive influence on the field during the games.

It was an honour to play alongside such a football legend. All the boys at Raith respected him and accepted his ways. Whenever we played a game, he would walk off the park at full time, shower, change and then was off away back to Dundee. He wasn't interested in the social side at the club. I can only assume he had done this his entire football career, so why change?

I have seen him a couple of times since we all retired at Raith, when we have been back at Kirkcaldy, and he hasn't changed one bit. He has turned 60 years old but still looks as fit as the day he walked away from Raith Rovers into retirement.

Playing Kilmarnock was going to be another tough game. They had some quality players and we knew this wasn't going to be easy. An old teammate from my St Mirren days, Tom Black, was in the opposing team. He was a very good footballer with a good left foot and he was an even better golfer. We knew Kilmarnock were not going to be pushovers but we had home advantage and the crowd behind us, so we knew if we put a shift in, we had a great chance of reaching the quarter-finals.

When the game arrived, there was a good attendance and a great atmosphere and it was set up nicely for us. The first thirty minutes flew by and we were being matched by Kilmarnock, and they scored from a corner to take a one-nil lead. At this point I was wondering what Davie Narey was thinking and whether he was starting to have regrets about finishing his career in Kirkcaldy. I didn't worry for long as almost immediately, we got back level with Mickey Cameron blasting in a goal for us from close range after some good play from Dazza and Ally Graham.

Our second goal came just before half-time and I was involved in it. I got the ball on the left and sent over a deep cross to Ally Graham. Ally did what he's good at and headed the ball towards Mickey Cameron, who hit a fantastic overhead kick that flew past Geddes. It was a brilliant goal from Mickey and a quality move put us two-one ahead. When we got in at halftime, the gaffer was busy chatting away like he did with all the enthusiasm he did with everything in life.

I always thought that if only Jimmy's character and enthusiasm could be bottled for us to share out every ninety minutes on a Saturday afternoon on the park, then we would have been world beaters. I suppose in a way it was, which is why the club did so well under Jimmy's management.

His buzz rubbed off on the team and we headed out for the second half looking to build on our lead. We went back onto the Starks Park pitch hoping to grab another goal early on and finish them off. The lads up front were playing well and looked like a quality partnership, with Dazza feeding off Ally Graham's headers and presence. Eventually, in the 77th minute, Davie Narey placed a free kick across to Ally Graham, who nodded the ball on and in came Mickey Cameron to put the ball past their keeper to secure his hat-trick, the second in the Coca Cola Cup from our team.

At 3-1 ahead, we thought the tie was over and we could just play the game out, but Kilmarnock showed a lot of character to get a goal back just two minutes later through Bobby Williamson. There was only ten minutes left and Ronnie Coyle was brought on to help keep our lead with an extra defender. It worked as we saw out the game. The final whistle blew and we were into the quarter-finals.

Our league form was still up and down, but being in the last eight of a cup competition was something to look forward to and we hoped that we'd get a good draw that might allow us to progress.

That proved to be the case as we were drawn against a fellow First Division side in St Johnstone. The game was away at McDairmid Park and they were a good side, but we knew that it gave us a chance to go further. We travelled up to Perth on the 20th September for what we knew would be a tough match. The manager had decided to play, which gave the lads a bit of a buzz. He was still technically a player-manager, but his appearances had been limited for the last year so he rarely played in the first team. I am not sure why he decided to play himself that night.

Perhaps he realised that the opportunity to get to a semi-final didn't come along too often for clubs like Raith Rovers and he might have been thinking that the best place to get his thoughts across to the team was on the pitch, right next to his players. He may have been older than the rest of us but he was still fit as a fiddle. When he had played before, you wouldn't have believed he was one of the older guys.

His enthusiasm on the pitch was like a young boy at Christmas who had just opened the best present ever. He could also play a bit. He would be running up and down in midfield, commanding that central area and knocking the ball about as if it was a training session. His enthusiasm rubbed off on you and you could not help but raise your game. So much so that I just wish he could have carried on for another season or two and I believe every player at Raith Rovers would say exactly the same.

We travelled up to Perth and the same old music is played as we approach the ground. Tina Turner's Simply the Best was our theme tune in those days, something Jimmy had borrowed from his previous club Rangers. It had been good to us so far, so why not. There was a great following of Rovers fans there packed in the stand behind the goal and the atmosphere felt very different to previous rounds.

It did feel as if the fans knew we were getting closer to the big one and the mood amongst the players was, 'This is it lads, concentrate and no messing about'. Not that we ever messed about in the other rounds, but I think we started to be aware that we were only two games away from a major final.

We get into the changing rooms and the usual fight for what music is played. The gaffer had the worst taste ever and Dazza's music taste wasn't too far behind him. The young lads like Stevie Crawford and Stevie McAnespie tended to get more air time that the rest of us, or perhaps they were just more prepared to bring along CD's all the time.

Inside the changing room, there were footballs and shirts and programmes laid out on the physio's table that needed signing. It seemed that the further we went in the competition; the more items were in the dressing room requiring signatures.

During the cup run, I had a strain that was causing me a lot of problems running. I don't think I ever told anybody about it as I didn't want to lose my place in the team. The competition was now fierce and we had one or two versatile players in our squad so I needed to keep it to myself. I felt I always had a bit of strange running style anyway, so even though I had to compensate for my injury, I thought nobody would be able to tell.

I suppose it could be seen as letting down the lads, the manager, and supporters, by not allowing somebody fitter to play, but we were on an amazing cup run and I desperately wanted to keep my place. I suspect most other players would have done the same. And if you asked any Raith Rovers fan, that if they had the chance to play for the club in the League Cup competition, but had a strain, what they would do, I bet they would play with it and hope they don't get found out. So not only did I have to worry about matching the St Johnstone right sided players, I had to worry about my performance with a strain that restricted my game.

The build-up before kick-off was more intense than usual and you could feel in the dressing room that the lads were meant business tonight. This was reinforced by the roar from our fans that had turned up in big numbers and were expecting a good performance. The game started well and we looked good, zipping the ball around, with Jimmy Nicholl leading the way. Ally Graham was playing well up front winning everything in the air, and combining with his strike partner Stevie Crawford, who had the pace to outrun most defenders. It was great playing under the lights.

I always loved playing under floodlights, as it gives that extra atmosphere to a game. The first goal came from an unlikely player in Shaun Dennis in the 19th minute. Jimmy Nicholl took a corner and it ended up at the back of the box, where Mickey Cameron passed it back into the box and there was Dennis, to head the ball into the back of the net. Big Shaun didn't score many goals in his career so that was probably up there as one of his most important. The Rover's support erupted when the ball hit the back of the net. It was only what we deserved, because at this point we were by far the better team.

Ten minutes later, we got our second. Jimmy Nicholl started the goal by a great run and lay off to Danny Lennon. Danny then tried to cross the ball over but it took a deflection which Mickey Cameron picked up and then picked out Ally on the penalty spot. Ally controlled beautifully and hammered it home in the roof of the net. After scoring a hat-trick against Ross County, Ally was having a brilliant cup run. Behind Scott Thomson's goal, the Rovers fans loved it, and at that point they must have already thought we were in the semi-final. We were dominant and had a two-goal cushion to take into the second half. We knew that our opponents were probably going to get a roasting by their manager at half-time.

In the dressing room at half-time, things were as they always were. The gaffer was trying to tell us to keep it going and Martin Harvey was going around as he always did in his quiet Irish manner talking to individuals one-to one. I did notice that there seemed to be a lot more people in the dressing room, and it felt a bit chaotic, but all I was thinking about was about my injury. My main thought was, 'how come nobody can see I am running with a one bad limb?'

I was worried, but figured if they cannot see it then I will just try to forget the dull ache and get on with it. The half-time period went fast and it was time to go back out again. There was one final gee up from everybody and out we went feeling confident but not complacent.

However, we were in for a shock as our opponents' mindset had clearly shifted and it only took five minutes for John O'Neil to strike back for Saints. He made a fine run into the box twisting and turning me and Sinky and hitting the ball through Thommo's legs. This was not what we had planned when discussing how to approach the second half. We knew they would get a massive lift scoring so quickly into the second half and that the game was far from over. For the next twenty minutes or so, the game was fairly even. We had chances and so did they.

Ally Graham had been magnificent throughout the cup run, but just when you thought he could not miss anything, he did by heading over Andy Rhodes crossbar from five yards out after a brilliant run and cross from Stevie Crawford. It was a chance to kill the game and I started to think that maybe our luck had changed. All it needed was for them to get one back and they would then be totally on the front foot and want to finish us off. But I know the lads that were around me.

They never give up and have a never say die attitude. When you have Mickey Cameron and Danny Lennon in your team, then there's always the chance we can score, and after riding our luck with a wave of St Johnstone attacks, that's exactly what we did with only seven minutes left of the match. Saints was now trying to pile the pressure on and there wasn't a lot of time left. As they pushed forward to get that equaliser, we broke.

Danny Lennon passed to Mickey and then carried on running. Mickey placed an astute ball back to Danny who ran on and blasted the ball past Rhodes who had come out to try and narrow the angle. Danny was there too quick for Rhodes and as soon as he scored, at our fans end of the stadium, things went crazy. The lads were jumping for joy and the supporters were going wild. We knew there was no coming back from the third goal. The rest of the game was played out and the final whistle blew. That's it, semi-final here we come!

Back in the changing rooms it was buzzing with more people than I had ever seen in one room. The feeling was fantastic. The trip home on the coach was brilliant, wondering who we would get in the next round and I'm sure some of us were starting to dream about reaching a major final. Life was good.

We were flying in the cup, but the league form continued to struggle. We were plodding along and slowly moving up the table, but quite a distance away from the top team at the time, Dunfermline. The distraction of the cup run might have been a hindrance or it might have been helping, it was hard to tell. When we were drawn against another First Division rival, Airdrie in the semi-final and managed to avoid the two Premier League teams, Celtic and Aberdeen, then we really started to believe we could make the final.

The week building up to the semi-final was quite hectic with the media around us wanting interviews. Thankfully, most of the interviewing was done by the younger lads and Gordon Dalziel. Dazza always liked the attention, which I was happy with as I could just concentrate on getting ready for the game.

Training remained the same. Jimmy Nicholl and Martin Harvey saw no reason to change it just because we were in a semi-final. We normally trained in a local park. The young YTS lads had to go up first to make sure it was clear of anything that wasn't good to step in or tread on, and to scare off any local stray dogs. Training was normally short but intense. The gaffer liked crossing and shooting and some tactics then ending it with a five-a-side.

The goalkeepers at the club liked to think they could score the goals and would take their chances playing up front. There was Scott Thomson, Ray Allan and Brian Potter. Brian was the sub-keeper who usually sat on the bench for first team games. Brian was a hard-working young man and he totally respected Scott Thompson in every way. They would often be training by themselves when the rest of the lads were busy on their own training. They built a good rapport together and Brian was a really nice down-to-earth person, who could be relied upon.

The gaffer persuaded the board members that, for such an important game, that they should spend some money and to take us away to a Hotel. I think he felt that we would be distracted by being at home with the family or maybe he just wanted to keep an eye on us all! The board agreed and we were fortunate to enjoy the delights of a secluded Hotel dating back to 1725 called The Nivingston House Hotel near Loch Leven for a few days before the game. The hotel was on some ghost listing website and rumoured to be haunted. Supposedly there was an old woman dressed in her nightwear that at night would walk around the hotel opening and closing bedroom doors. It is also said that she spends a lot of time in one of the bedrooms that the former owner shot himself in around the 1900s.

The story goes that Jimmy Nicholl went down to see the night porter because he thought there was a cold presence inside his bed. The night porter replied to the gaffer, that he better sign the guest book as this has occurred many times before. The porter went on to say that there are often strange happenings in the hotel that cannot be explained. These stories were told to some of the lads when we arrived and you can imagine it was a red rag to a bull for some of the boys to wind others up.

The word got around and it didn't take long before one or two of them were hiding behind doors and curtains then jumping out on the others to frighten them. This happened to Sinky, the so called tough centre half. He got so frightened when Danny Lennon jumped out behind the curtains that he ran down the hallway the fastest he had ever run in his life.

The following morning, we were all sat down for breakfast and Dazza and Ally Graham were telling the story that during the night, they saw a shadowy figure at the end of their beds, and this was confirmed by the hotel manager. Surely these two big centre forwards didn't call for the manager to come up to their bedroom?

During the short stay at the hotel, we were all allowed a night out to have a few beers, but to be back by 12:30am. We were in the middle of nowhere so we asked the hotel manager and he said the nearest place that had a pub was a small place called Kinross. The decision was made.

We all went to Kinross and chilled out in a pub chatting away about the game and anything else to ease any pressure that might be building. Time passed and we soon realised that it was midnight and if we didn't get back to the hotel on time then we would be fined. Panic set in as it came to light that there were only two taxis in Kinross so not all of us could get back by the deadline the gaffer had set. If my memory serves me right, Thommo went knocking on random doors in Kinross asking if anybody would give them a lift back to the hotel.

Incredibly, one local said yes and we managed to get back in time to avoid a fine. It was every man for themselves by then so as we passed Shaun Dennis and a few of the other lads in the street, we shouted at them to get a move on or else they would be fined. I never found out if they got back in time as twenty minutes later, Thommo was making me a nice brew and tucking me into my bed!

The word got around that the club had sold all the 5500 tickets allocated to our supporters, so we knew it was going to be a fantastic atmosphere in the ground. We boarded the coach to make the short trip up to Perth. The coach trip was exactly the same as all the other trips with some dodgy music playing in the background, some of the lads deep in concentration and the rest of us playing cards. When we arrived for the evening kick off, it was clear that a lot of the fans had arrived early to the ground just in case of delays. It had been 45 years since the club had last been in a final so they didn't want to miss out. That, coupled with the fact that Raith Rovers hadn't won a major trophy in 111 years, meant that there was a lot of pressure on us to do the job.

Typical of Raith Rovers, it wasn't until we got to the stadium, that Jimmy Nicholl realised somebody was missing. The gaffer went over to Martin Harvey and said that somebody is missing and not sure who. They then realised that they had left Davie Narey at the hotel. Now I know Davie can be a quiet man but for nobody to realise that he was missing during the coach trip is amazing.

Martin Harvey said that he mistakenly thought Jimmy had given Davie permission to travel up in his car as we were reasonably close to Dundee, where the big defender lived. They called the hotel and the response was that the hotel chef is on his way up with Davie in his car. I am not sure if the chef got to stay and watch the match. I hope he did as it was the least he deserved.

It was just before we had to go out for kick-off and the ghetto blaster in the dressing room was turned off and Jimmy Nicholl gave his final speech to us to get us motivated. It was a semi-final and we were all aware of exactly what was at stake so there wasn't much need for extra motivation. If a semi-final doesn't get you going then it's time to give up. After Jimmy finished, we got up and shook each other's hands, gave each other a pat on the back or said a few words to each other. We left the dressing room with the noise of everybody in the room cheering each other on to go out and do the business.

We walked out on the field and the majority of the crowd were Raith fans. That was a boost as it felt more of a home game to us. As I was warming up before we kicked off, I spoke briefly to my old teammate from my Barnsley days, Stevie Cooper. Stevie played up front for Airdrie and was a superb athlete. I had never seen anybody better in the air than Stevie. He trained as a gymnast as a kid, and when he used to score for Barnsley, he would do several back flips which the fans loved to see.

We wished each other all the best, but on this occasion, I knew I wanted my team to be the best. Airdrie were no pushovers and every time I had played against them, you knew it was always going to be a battle. They played hard and were a disciplined team. We had belief though. We had the talent in our side to scare any team in Scotland and I never had any doubts about the younger lads in our team. We can do this.

The game started and as expected, it's fast and furious. We are on top early with a few chances from Cameron, Dalziel and Graham. It was a great start to the first half but we needed that goal that our play deserved. It arrived in the 39th minute. Davie Narey got a nosebleed when he went forward from midfield and eventually joined a scramble at the edge of the box.

The Airdrie defender tried to walk the ball out of their area but Narey intercepted the ball and it ended up at the feet of Dazza. Dazza squared it across to his strike partner, Ally Graham, who blasted it past John Martin. We had the lead and the lads were jumping all over Ally but I just walked slowly back to my position at the left of defence as I needed to preserve my energy. I was still carrying the strain and I could feel it all the time, but was not going to tell anybody especially now.

I was grimacing, but none of my teammates or the backroom staff seemed to notice. I was aware that if we were four goals up and there was no reason to carry on, then I would have called to the bench and come off just as a precaution. But for now, we were one up and things were going well.

The first half ended and we went back to the dressing room full of confidence. Having taken the lead, we knew we were now a little closer to the magical cup final but there was still a long way to go. The gaffer obviously felt the same as his half-time talk was routine, basically telling us to keep it going and to get another goal and finish them off. We returned to the pitch buzzing to get the job done.

The game was to take a dramatic turn in the 69th minute. We had coped well up until then and even though Airdrie had stepped up a gear trying to get the goal to draw level, we were managing to repel all of the Airdrie attack. A routine long ball over our defence looked to be causing us no problems. Thommo came out to collect but realised he had stepped outside of his box. He quickly tried to get back into the box as he took hold of the long ball from Jimmy Boyle.

The linesman made the decision that he had caught the ball outside his area and therefore, had to be sent off. You can imagine how we felt in that moment. We were comfortable and heading towards a cup final and now we were being reduced to ten men. We were all over the ref, and Thommo was pleading his innocence to anyone who would listen. The Airdrie fans and team were doing the opposite and shouting for the goalkeeper to be sent off. They got their demands. Thommo had to go, and off he walked. He was my roommate and friend and having never been sent off before, I knew how bad he would be feeling.

We now had a major problem because, not only were we playing the last 30 minutes with one player less but we needed to substitute an outfield player to get another keeper on. The decision was made quickly by the manager to sacrifice Davie Kirkwood in order to get Brian Potter on. We were all aware that 'Potts' was very young and had only played one game in the first team the previous season, a meaningless end of season kick about against Dundee United.

But we also knew there was no other choice. The young 'keeper was being put in at the deep end and we knew we would be up against it until full time. I can only imagine the stress Potts would be feeling. The first thing he had to do was to be ready for a free kick to them just at the edge of the box. He was in the goals that were in front of the Airdrie supporters, so they were giving him some stick. It took a few minutes for the keepers to swap and for everybody to get ready for the direct free kick. Kenny Black took the free kick and fortunately when he struck it, the ball deflected from our wall, away just enough to miss the goals. I knew now we would be under tremendous pressure from now on, but still had faith that we could do it, if we got the breaks. The gaffer decided to put Ally Graham in the defence and we hoped to defend well enough to get to full time with the one-nil win.

The notion of holding on to our lead lasted only another five minutes as Airdrie drew level. My old teammate, Stevie Cooper, picked up the ball 20 yards out and hit the perfect volley into the net. It was a fantastic strike and I doubt any keeper would have stopped it. It was possibly the goal of the season and the last thing we needed. They were now on the front foot and all we could do it get through the ninety minutes without conceding. We were so much in control and then one incident turned the game upside down. Thankfully, we survived for the rest of the second half, but only just, and reached extra-time.

I decided that it was time for me to come off as I was shattered and I was feeling my injuries. I knew that if we could hold out in extra time, that it was better to have fit and able lads ready for the penalties, and I was not one, so I asked to be brought off. I was replaced with Jason Rowbotham, who was an excellent player, very versatile and a potential penalty taker.

The extra time period was mainly backs to the wall with some brilliant defending by us. We did get the odd chance but it was mainly Airdrie trying to break us down, but with a little luck and great teamwork, we got through it and survived. It was down to penalties. The lads were on the pitch when the gaffer and Martin Harvey came to them and selected the boys to take the spot kicks.

They were Shaun Dennis, Stevie Crawford, Danny Lennon, Steve McAnespie and Colin Cameron. The penalties were to be taken at the end where the Airdrie supporters were, which I didn't like, but then we won the toss of the coin and opted to go first.

Shaun Dennis was the first to take his penalty and up he strolled and got himself ready for the ref to blow his whistle to take his kick. I was in our dug-out and basically couldn't watch so I had to wait for our fans to roar with joy to know if we had scored or if Airdrie had missed. So, any memories I have of the actual penalties are from watching the DVD after the game! Shaun took a decent penalty, placing it the wrong way of John Martin and gave us a great start.

The next batch of penalties were all scored with Jimmy Boyle, Steve McAnespie, Andy Smith, Mickey Cameron and Paul Jack all successfully hitting the back of the net. The score was 3-3 and we were waiting for someone to make a mistake. The pressure on the lads was incredible by now, as every player had scored and I would have hated to be there waiting to take a penalty kick. I was impressed that these guys had the balls to step up.

Next for us was Stevie Crawford who walked all the way from the halfway line just like the others had done. I cannot imagine what was going through his mind while he was walking towards the ball. Stevie takes his penalty and manages to score again. It is now four-three and getting to the crucial spot kicks. Airdrie's Kenny Black confidently takes his penalty and makes it level again.

The last penalty kick for us was being taken by Danny Lennon. Danny was our captain and a real leader and you wouldn't have wanted anyone else taking our final penalty. He scored to give us the lead 5-4 and place all the pressure on the last Airdrie penalty taker, Alan Lawrence. We knew that if he misses then that's it. As he walked up, I couldn't watch and neither could Gordon Dalziel.

I think by that stage we were both half way down the tunnel! We waited and then heard this tremendous roar from the Rover's support and we knew that Lawrence has missed. Dazza and I looked towards the pitch and all we could see was the lads sprinting towards Brian Potter and jumping all over him and then Rovers fans coming onto the pitch in their thousands.

We had won. Raith Rovers were in the Coca Cola Cup Final. What a feeling. I went onto the pitch to celebrate with the boys and the supporters, but I couldn't get near Brian. He was being carried along on somebody's shoulders. It was wonderful to see him having his moment.

I decided to get back towards the tunnel and back to the dressing room. When I got inside, it was bedlam. You couldn't move for people and the champagne was flowing already and all the lads were embracing and the club staff and directors were hugging each other. After the chaos, we got showered and dried and out onto the coach to head back home. The journey back down to Fife was fantastic.

Everybody was having fun, some drinking beer, some drinking champagne but everybody had a smile on their faces. I wish that coach journey home could have lasted all night. I am not sure if I went out with all the lads into Kirkcaldy that night or if I just went home. Things were a blur, but it was a great game and a great night and a moment in my career that I am truly proud of. Brian Potter was the hero that night and he deserves all the credit going for getting us to a cup final.

Chapter Eleven: Build up to the Final

"Autumn shows us how beautiful it is to let things go"

The build up to the cup final was both wonderful and awful for me. I was going through a very difficult time as my Mother was gravely ill and passed away on the 7th November 1994.Margaret Hilda Broddle had spent her entire life working hard and then raising her family and her loss was a major blow.

At the time, I had just moved into a brand-new house near Dalgety Bay, that the Raith Rovers chairman Alex Penman had built for me. Our telephone line had not been installed yet so when I had a long conversation to have, I would have to walk to the village telephone box. I can remember just before she passed away, calling her from that phone box and not realising just how bad her cancer had got.

She had kept the worst of it hidden from me, but as we were talking away, she broke down and was crying on the other end of the phone. My mum or Dad were not emotional people through their life, so I knew by how upset she was that something was really bad. What I can remember about the conversation was my mum giving me encouragement and telling me to 'go and win the cup'.

On the night of the 6th November we went with the kids to a local public bonfire, and I received a call to get home quick, as my mum was in a bad way in the Rotherham General Hospital. I set off in the car for South Yorkshire immediately. The weather was terrible with severe fog and I had to drive slowly all the way along the A1.

The journey felt like it took forever, but I finally got there and went straight to the Hospital. As I entered her room, she had just passed away before I could say my last goodbyes. I was so angry and frustrated that had it not been so foggy that night, then I would have there much quicker and I could have spoken to her one last time.

I called Jimmy Nicholl and stayed in Yorkshire for a couple of days before having to go back to Scotland to prepare for the final. I went back a few days later for the funeral and my mum was buried at our beautiful village church in Laughton. All the family were very upset as you could imagine, but I had no tears.

When people asked why, I told them that I had been made aware my mum was riddled with cancer and in tremendous pain, the hospital staff had to pump morphine into her to ease the pain, so while I was very upset to have lost her, I was delighted she was now had relief from her pain and could now look over us all and keep an eye on us from above. God bless you Mum.

The build up to the final against Celtic was crazy. Alongside the training and match preparation, the club had constant media attention. Almost every day for the three weeks before the final, there were reporters wanting an interview or there would be a photographer wanting pictures for their paper. The decision was made very early to play down our chances of winning the final. Whenever the manager or the lads were asked their opinion, we all said we will give it a damn good try but we are the underdogs and realistically we are not expected to win. We all hoped that when the Celtic lads read the papers that they would actually believe the stories and take it for granted that they just had to turn up on the day to claim the trophy.

We still had the league to contend with too, and we were now playing well and creeping up the table getting closer to the top two teams. I think it helped that we were all fighting for a starting place in the final. If you were in the first team, then you had to make sure you performed well to keep your place and then a place in the final would come your way too. The three games before the final had been won comfortably, including a 3-0 win in the last game against Clydebank away. I remember that game that the whole squad was just brimming with confidence.

It was a winning feeling that you only experienced on rare occasions. The lads played so well and it was just the tonic we needed before the final. I am sure that Celtic would have people watching us that day, and when they sent their report back to Tommy Burns and his team, it would have put a little bit of doubt into the Celtic minds, or at the very least got them thinking.

Celtic is a huge club and always expected to win trophies but they hadn't won anything in five years and the pressure was on. Their support demanded success and the fact that their last two games were average and they could only draw and finding it hard to score wouldn't have helped either.

I tried to not think about the game too much and tried to play it down in my own mind. Firstly, nobody knew who would be getting a starting place, and secondly, it was possible that during training or the league games before that I might get injured. When I got through the Clydebank game without any further strain on my existing injuries, it was a great relief.

I knew that I had the added pressure of Jason Rowbotham fighting for my place, and there's no doubt that Jason was a good player and popular amongst the lads. He was dependable, versatile and also a penalty taker. However, I had played all season and hoped that Jimmy Nicholl would keep the same team as we had almost all season, particularly as we were playing so well.

The build-up went well for the squad with one major exception. Our captain, Danny Lennon, sustained an injury in training that ruled him out for the final. It was just a normal training session, and an accident which could happen to anybody at any time, but as he had been a major influence throughout the tournament, we were all gutted for him. He deserved to be in that team and enjoy that moment in his career, but with him side-lined, we knew we had to try our hardest to win the cup for our captain.

The club organised for us to stay in a Hotel in Erskine for the three days before the final. I would be rooming with Scott Thomson as usual, and although we tried to everything as normal, I could feel the pressure building up a little by now. We trained close to the hotel for one session and then with the influence of Jimmy Nicholl, were allowed access to train at Ibrox where the final would be played.

Cup finals in Scotland are usually played at Hampden Park, but it was being upgraded at the time, so the switch was made to the home of Rangers FC. Jimmy Nicholl was a former Rangers legend and his old club couldn't do enough for us.

We had full access to their facilities, and they even advised to wear a certain stud in our football boots as the pitch had recently been re-laid. We trained at Ibrox and were all acting as if it was just another training day, but we all knew that this would be one of the biggest games in our lives. It was only natural to feel anxious and be wondering if you had done enough to secure your place in the team.

Most of the lads weren't told if they were in the team until the day of the game itself, but the young lads Stevie Crawford, Mickey Cameron and Jason Dair were all asked to see the gaffer the night before the final and told they would in the line-up to face Celtic. It was a brave decision to start with such youth, but they were all great talents and deserved their place. All three were told not to say anything as the rest of would be told the team the following morning. The

night before the game was a Saturday and most of us were in this room at the hotel relaxing, playing cards, quizzes and darts. There was a knock on the door and in came a waiter with several beers that had been ordered by the gaffer. Most managers would frown upon drinking before a game, never mind a major cup final. But Jimmy Nicholl knew how the lads ticked. It gave some light relief and took the pressure off, another genius idea from Jimmy Nicholl.

The following day was Sunday 27th November, 1994. It would be one of the greatest days of my life, but first thing that morning I still didn't know whether I had a place in the starting eleven or not. After breakfast, we were asked to gather by the gaffer and the nerves kicked in. Would I be handed the opportunity to play in a major cup final or was I destined to miss out? It felt like my whole career had been building to this point. From starting out as young lad at Sheffield United and then moving on to my other clubs in Scunthorpe, Barnsley, Plymouth, St Mirren and Partick Thistle. I felt this was likely to be my only chance to feature in a cup final. Even though I knew I had played just about every game since the start of the season, I still needed to hear my name called out. I thought back to the disappointments of the past, managers who didn't like my face, being sold by Barnsley when I wanted to stay, the periods of self-doubt when I struggled to find form. I took nothing for granted.

We gathered in one of the meeting rooms at the hotel and the manager stood up to read out the team.

'Thomson, McAnespie, Broddle...'

To my great relief, I was in. That's all I was interested in at that point. I could gather my thoughts and listen to the rest of the team to see who else was in and who had been left out altogether.

'...Narey, Dennis, Sinclair, Crawford, Dalziel, Graham, Cameron and Dair, Substitutes: Rowbotham, Redford and Potter.'

Football is slightly a selfish job. Sometimes your main focus is yourself. There wasn't the money there is in the game nowadays so being in the team meant not only that you had the chance to play, but if you played well, it put you in prime position for the next game, win bonus, and appearance money.

We weren't megastars and were paid like the best electrician or plumber at the time, so the extras came from win bonuses and other incentives were important. I still had a young family and a house to pay for, so I had to get in that team to help bring in the extra money I needed to make life that little bit more comfortable. So, at times your focus was keep yourself in the team and keep others out. I was in and I could now relax a little more and commiserate with the lads that didn't make it.

After announcing the team, the gaffer then gave a speech like no other. All that was missing was the Dambusters music in the background and it would have been perfect. That got us all choked and ready to take on anybody put in front of us. I can't remember exactly what was said, but if you can think of the best speech you have ever heard from a movie, then you are halfway there.

It was soon time to leave for Ibrox. Scott Thomson and I went back to our room and got ourselves ready and packed up. Then it was down to the reception where some supporters were waiting for us to wish us good luck. We boarded the coach for the twenty-minute trip into Glasgow. During the journey, I felt we were not as boisterous as usual, but I think that was because most of us just wanted to take it all in.

The music was blasting as we got closer to the stadium and looking out of the windows, we watched all the fans mingling together carrying their team flags and scarves. There were a lot of fans at the ground early and our supporters were waving and clapping us as we drove slowly along towards the ground. We finally arrived and entered the ground, and after the initial walk into the home changing room, it was out onto the pitch to soak up that atmosphere and check out the pitch. There were already some fans inside the ground and we had a round of applause from the Rover's section as we came on to the pitch.

Once I got back into the dressing room I sat down to have a read of the programme. I have always tried to get every programme for every game I played in professionally and have them all in my garage or inside scrapbooks. This one was special and I knew that win or lose it would be something that I would treasure all my life. So there was no way I was going to let anybody have my programme that day.

It was getting closer to kick off, so it was time to get changed and put the cup final kit on. The kit was brand new and had the cup final details embroidered in it. There was even a spare one, one long sleeve and one short sleeve. They were another great memento of the day.

I always got my legs massaged by Gerry Docherty with deep heat and oil, and aside from the strains I was carrying, I was feeling ok. I put on the full strip and it was back outside for the warm-up. I wasn't one for running around unless told to when warming up. I always thought it was wasting energy that I desperately needed for the actual match! So, as usual, I did enough to keep management and coaches happy then it was back into the changing room.

There was one last message from Jimmy Nicholl in the dressing room but it was brief as he had said all he needed to say back at the hotel. It was then time to walk out in front of 45,000 supporters and play in one of my most important games in my 17-year career. I walked out third in the team line-up, throwing ball up and down, as I emerged from the tunnel and into the incredible noise of both sets of fans. I was ready for the game to start.

Chapter Twelve:
27/11/94

"Don't wait for the perfect moment. Take the moment and make it perfect"

The game kicks off and in no time, I got a sliding tackle in against Mike Galloway. From then on, the game went in favour to us, at least in the early stages. The boys were doing well and I felt the younger ones were too quick and full of energy for the Celtic midfield. They wanted to be able to look up and play the ball but our young, energetic players wouldn't allow them time.

After just a few minutes, Stevie Crawford used his pace to put the ball past Celtic defender Tony Mowbray, and the response by Mowbray was to take Stevie out. It was a cynical tackle that if it hadn't been so early in the game then Mowbray should have been sent off. I think everybody watching on TV and in the stadium, that wasn't a Celtic supporter, would agree. Mowbray being the experienced professional defender knew exactly what he was doing and got away with it. The referee, Jim McCluskey, only gave him a booking.

It was a great start and made Celtic realise it was going to be a tough game for them. We knew everybody in the media thought Celtic were favourites, and rightly so, but we had total belief in ourselves as a team and not as individuals, and this had carried us all the way to the final. The noise of the fans continued to echo around the stands and they were in for one of the best League Cup finals in many a year, if not the best.

The first 15 minutes went quickly. Mickey Cameron had two good chances and then just before the 19th minute, we earned a corner. It was my responsibility to take the corner. I walked towards the far corner and could see a wall of Celtic fans in the stand behind the goal. All I wanted to do was place a driven cross between the six-yard box and eighteen-yard box and not mess it up.

So, what do I do, I only manage to get it just above ground level but somehow it finds its way to Stevie Crawford and, fortunately for me, it makes the cross look like it was meant to be delivered that way. Stevie then turns a Celtic defender, put it's between his legs and hits it hard towards their goal. I watch from the corner as the ball sails past their goalkeeper Marshall and into the net.

We are one nil up in a major final against Celtic! Stevie runs over to the corner flag area and takes a Klinsmann like dive towards the Raith fans, who by now are jumping up and down like they had just won the lottery. The noise of the Raith Rovers fans in the Govan stand was simply amazing. It was a great start to the final and a very special moment.

We got back to our side of the field and Celtic started the game again. They meant business after the goal and came on strong. They were putting pressure on us and the game changed altogether. Celtic were now dominant and I could feel their constant threat. I was starting to think that I wish we had scored in the last minute of the game rather than so early! Our lead lasted only twelve minutes in the end. It took until the 32nd minute for Celtic to reply and it was Andy Walker who got the goal via a header, with our defence pulled apart by the relentlessness of the Celtic onslaught. The game had changed for the worst as far as we were concerned. Celtic had moved up a gear and we started to struggle.

The Celtic fans were buoyed by the equaliser and were generating an incredible level of noise. We knew we just had to ride it out and get to half-time. When the whistle finally went the relief amongst the Rovers players was palpable. I was grateful for halftime to arrive. We needed a breather and to get our game back in focus. The break allowed the gaffer and Martin Harvey a chance to get us back on track.

We left the changing room for the second half positive again and knew our strong bond would help us through and, with some magic from one of the lads we still might just do it. These lads had the ability to change games, and I was relying on them to do it for me. I had promised my Mum that we would win the cup, and in my mind, it had to happen for her.

I would like to think from the kick off that we matched them in every department, but if I am honest, when they came forward, they looked menacing and we needed a little luck to keep us level. Don't get me wrong, we still played some good football and created some chances, particularly as the game wore on. Mickey Cameron was having a fantastic game and they just couldn't handle him.

The game was edging towards the last quarter and it got to the fateful 84th minute. A great Celtic move ended up with the ball in the back of our net. I was deeply frustrated by the goal. The original shot hit the post and came back out to Nicholas instead of usually out for by kick when hitting the post at that angle.

Nicholas stunned us and the Celtic players embraced him as if he had just won them the cup. You couldn't help but feel that they thought it was over. Their supporters were now in full voice and, legend has it that the green and white ribbons were already being put on the trophy. With only six minutes left, there seemed to be no way back. Our opponents hadn't accounted for the fact that we were Raith Rovers and we play to the end.

We kicked off again with only a short time left and we gave everything we had. We started to pressure them immediately and we were knocking the ball about. Then in the 86th minute, Jason Dair received the ball from Sinky. Jason then took the ball inside his right position and struck the ball way outside of the 18-yard box. Gordon Marshall panicked and didn't take hold of the ball but instead fumbled the ball and out the ball came towards Dazza who was doing his usual and waiting for scraps inside the box.

The moment seemed to standstill as Dazza put his head to the ball and in it went, back of the net and we have scored. This game was fairytale stuff. The Raith fans went crazy again and the Celtic fans couldn't believe it. What a match and what a goal. It was now two goals each. I was delighted that we had got the goal we deserved.

I had that really positive feeling now. This team never gives up. We can do this. This late goal would give us the lift we needed. Let extra time come and we will go on to win. The Celtic players were devastated and looked exhausted.

Shortly after, it was full time and extra time was needed. We stayed on the park and Jimmy Nicholl and the rest of the staff came on too. While the gaffer was giving his team talk, I was exhausted and thinking would my body and legs hold out? Extra-time started and we immediately were knocking the ball about and keeping the ball away from Celtic. It was a great start and I was enjoying myself, until I had to run for a ball to see it out and I stretched and the strained leg went.

That was it. I immediately gave a sign to the dugout that I needed to be replaced. There were 93 minutes on the large stadium clock and my game was over. I was replaced by Jason Rowbotham. I like to think I had done my bit and now it was over to a fresh player in Jason. He deserved to get a game as he was such a consistent performer for the team when he played. I got to the dugout and put this ridiculous thick jumpsuit on and tried to watch the game. It was tough sitting there and not be able to do anything more. At the back of my mind I was thankful that I was off the field, because if it did go to penalties then, to be truthful, I didn't fancy being asked to take one.

The rest of extra time went fast and although in the early stages we looked the better team, it slowly got to the point where most of the players were shattered and the football got slower and slower. It looked like neither team wanted to lose during the two periods and had settled for a penalty shootout. Gordon Dalziel came off before the end and so did Charlie Nicholas.

The early pace of the game was taking its toll on both sides and Stevie Crawford went down with cramp. It was understandable as he had run his heart out that day on the field. What a player. The extra time came and went and the ref blew his whistle. The destination of the cup was to be decided on penalties.

It struck me at the final whistle how different the two sets of supporters reacted at the result. The Raith Rovers faithful were very appreciative of what we had achieved and greeted the final whistle with cheers and applause. We knew we had given our all and the supporters accepted this. I am not sure the Celtic fans felt the same. They were clearly frustrated by the result and some of them let their team know it.

We got together on the field, just as we had done in the semi-final and Jimmy Nicholl picked his players to take the penalties. The penalty takers for us would be Shaun Dennis, Jason Dair, Colin Cameron, Stevie Crawford, and Steve McAnespie. There were a few hugs and shaking hands and then it was time to leave the field and it was left to the selected few. The penalties followed a similar pattern to the semi-final against Airdrie with everyone scoring in the early stages.

First up again, was Shaun Dennis. One – Nil

Willie Falconer equalised for Celtic. One – One

Jason Dair was next for us, Two – One

John Collins next for Celtic. Two - Two

Mickey Cameron slotted in the next. Three - Two.

Andy Walker for Celtic. Three - Three

Stevie Crawford, who had recovered from his cramp was next for us. Four - Three

Paul Byrne for Celtic. Four - Four

The tension was rising with each successful kick, with each player knowing that a mistake at this stage would be critical to their hopes of lifting the trophy.

Steve McAnespie took out fifth penalty. Five - Four

Mike Galloway stepped up for Celtic. He hit a relatively poor shot and Scott Thomson managed to get across to it, but frustratingly the ball squirmed under his body and into the net. Five - Five

Every player that had volunteered had stepped up and under incredible pressure, scored. It was now sudden death.

Jason Rowbotham stepped up to take the next penalty. It was a cracker. Six - Five.

We looked to see who was next for Celtic and it was their captain, Paul McStay.

Paul was one of the nicest guys you could meet. He was captain of Celtic and had all the added pressure of knowing that if he missed then there wasn't another chance.

As McStay approached the penalty area, Thommo decided to throw the ball high in the air just as Brian Potter had done in the semi-final. The Celtic player then placed the ball on the penalty spot and tried to calm himself and wait for the referees' whistle. The ref blew and Paul struck the ball. Thommo dived the right way and saved!

Unbelievably, we were the Coca Cola League Cup winners!

Everybody involved in the club ran onto the pitch to the noise and roar of the Raith Rovers supporters. I had a pulled leg muscle so it was difficult to run but I didn't care, I had to get on that field to celebrate with the lads.

As I started to run, Jimmy Nicholl, who had already got a head start on me suddenly stopped, then turned around and looked towards me. We grabbed each other in total joy and happiness. It was a special moment with a special man, the man who had guided Raith Rovers to their first ever major

trophy. We finished our impromptu embrace and ran towards the rest of the lads and after then, I cannot quite remember the rest. It was a total blur of disbelief. All I could think about was my Mum and my children. The kids were very young at the time but they were there with Jan watching. And then my mum, I knew that had she been there watching then she would have been very proud of her youngest son.

The celebrations after the final penalty kick was saved were an amazing feeling. We could tell that the supporters were enjoying it just as much as we were. We were ecstatic, although all the lads had run in different directions. When we finally all came together it was a great moment. We looked around the stadium, many of the lads in shock, and couldn't believe how few Celtic fans were left. The Celtic ends of the ground had emptied. It was as if they had been transported away in seconds by that Star Trek teleporter.

While we were waiting, and celebrating with the Raith Rovers supporters, I was asked to give an interview on the football pitch live to the BBC cameras. It was Chick Young doing the interview who I knew reasonably well from my St Mirren days. I don't remember much about the interview as I have never seen it, but over the years a number of fans have told me that my interview was excellent, how well-spoken I was and how calm I came across.

Perhaps my training years earlier as a Sheffield United apprentice came in handy after all! I just wish I could play as well as I interviewed. I think when Chick had interviewed Ally Graham and Jimmy Nicholl prior to me, it was if they in shock and lost for words.

Eventually, the ribbons of blue and white were put on the trophy and the stand was placed in the middle of the football pitch for us to receive the trophy and medals. Gordon Dalziel was obviously the Captain and took hold of the trophy and raised it high towards the Raith fans and an almighty cheer erupted when he did. Once the handshakes and medals were handed to each player, we all went over to our supporters and just enjoyed the moment with them.

Raith Rovers had waited 111 years to win a major trophy and we knew this occasion and moment would remain their memories for many years to come. We had just made history and it was hard to take in.

Slowly, we made our way to the changing rooms where the champagne was waiting for us along the rest of the staff and directors of the club. It was just crazy and wonderful in there and something I will never forget. Even the Rangers Legend Ally McCoist came into the changing room to congratulate his old friend, Jimmy Nicholl. He was beaming with joy for us. Plus, that fact we had beaten Celtic was a massive bonus to him.

We then took showers and baths enjoying the moment and then got dressed and went out looking for our families. My two children were there with my wife Jan, and the in-laws all waiting for me. It was fantastic to see them and I felt so proud. I had a quick chat with them and then it was time to get on the bus and make our way back to Kirkcaldy and to the Dean Park Hotel, where there was a party waiting for us. I wasn't thinking about how was I going to get home after the party and how to get my family there, but I am sure that the details would sort themselves out.

The journey back to Fife was as perfect a trip as you could imagine. The drinks were flowing, the music was on and everybody was just buzzing. It was so good to be with your mates soaking up that special moment, and knowing that right now, there will be thousands of people from Kirkcaldy celebrating

along with us. We eventually got back to the hotel, and there appeared to be hundreds of supporters waiting for us. I am not sure how they found out where we were going but they did. I think they must have all tried to get into the hotel and if it had been down to me, I would have let them all in.

We made our way into the hotel and the Chairman, Alex Penman, told me that drinks and food and everything else was on the club. Well, you can imagine the delight when that news got around the boys. It was going to be a long but brilliant night. I was shattered after the long day and the efforts of the game but the promise of a free night was the pick me up to get me going again. Jan's mum Jean kindly agreed to stay at home with the kids and that meant that Jan, her father, Robbie, and I could enjoy the night. It was great to be able to celebrate our victory with them. We were placed at a table with a few of the lads and other close people to the club, and then the trophy was passed around to everybody to take a drink of champagne from it. You can imagine how many photographs were taken of every person sipping from the trophy. The night was just a very special night. Jan and I managed to blag a room at the hotel, although I don't know exactly who paid for it. Before everybody started to make their moves home, Jimmy Nicholl gathered us all together and told us that we had a game in the league the following Saturday. It was Sunday night and he said 'just enjoy ourselves, be careful, but be back in training by Wednesday'. I think some of the lads took full advantage of that and celebrated for a few days before getting back to the serious stuff of trying to catch Dunfermline and Dundee in the league.

There was once an English commentator who stupidly didn't know that Raith Rovers play in the coastal town of Kirkcaldy and that there wasn't actually a place called Raith.

He famously coined the phrase 'They will be dancing in the streets of Raith'. Although it was totally wrong, it has now become something the people of Kirkcaldy have taken to their hearts. The DVD of our exploits in the cup, which would be produced much later, took that name for its title. I liked to think that on 27th November 1994, it was the greatest night of dancing that Kirkcaldy had ever seen.

The following day we returned home and there were several telephone calls from reporters wanting more interviews. I was feeling a little rough, but got through them hopefully not sounding too stupid. I enjoyed the days off and it was so nice to be able to go shopping and do everyday stuff with the family.

Everywhere we went people came up to me and congratulated me on winning the League Cup, even some of the local Dunfermline supporters who were our biggest rivals. From that point on, anytime I went into Kirkcaldy, I felt I could have had free beer and stay at anybody's house if I asked. It was like having the keys to Kirkcaldy.

Wednesday came around quickly and it was back to work again. I think some of the lads were still hungover but it was great to see them all again. We got changed and made our way to the training ground. Waiting for us was a TV crew who were doing a DVD on the journey of winning the League Cup. We had to pretend that we were training before the final. We had won the cup but we had to train as if we hadn't even played the final yet. As you can imagine, it felt a little strange trying to look serious and pretending to listen to the gaffer doing a team talk on our last day training before the final. Later on, there were further pictures to be taken of the lads back at Stark's Park pouring champagne into the trophy for other media and press people.

The training that Wednesday was fun but a waste of time as I think all the lads and the manager were still on a high from the final.

It was a wonderful time to be a Raith Rovers player and I will cherish every moment. However, as the manager tried to impress upon us, we had an away game to Ayr United to prepare for and we needed to get back to work for the marathon of climbing the league and winning the points that would take us back to the Premier League.

Chapter Thirteen: Back to Business

"Trust before you love, know before you judge, commit before you promise, forgive before you forget and appreciate before you regret"

We had won the League Cup and had some time to savour the moment, but we knew that the main goal that gaffer had set us was to win the league and regain our place in the Premier League. The League Cup win may be a moment that will live on for the rest of my life, but back then it was a distraction from the real task in hand.

We had Ayr United to play away on Saturday 3rd December 1994 and were looking to kick start our First Division campaign. Most of the lads were still basking in the glory of the previous Sunday and not thinking about the league, but it was Jimmy Nicholl's job to get us back on track. We probably would have got away with not getting promoted from the Raith fans after winning the cup, but we wanted promotion and had to put the cup exploits out of our heads and concentrate on the rest of the season.

We trained as normal the rest of the week and then travelled over for the Ayr United game. When we came onto the football pitch just before kick-off, the Ayr United players had lined up in a guard of honour and clapped us onto the field. I thought that was a wonderful gesture and it has always stuck in my mind all these years after. I have the greatest respect to Ayr United for doing that and it showed the bond between footballers at that level who recognised the scale of our achievement.

The game itself was nothing special but ended up a 1-1 draw with Gordon Dalziel scoring for us. It was a start and at least we didn't get beat. We knew that given our league position that too many draws were not good enough as we had only half a season left to catch Dundee and Dunfermline. It was going to be tough, but we believed it was possible and at the very least, were ready to give it our best effort.

From that match, we started to gain in confidence. We lost to Airdrie but then went on a 14-match unbeaten run, with most of them wins. The belief was flowing through the team. We had beaten Celtic in a cup final so we started to believe that we could beat anybody. This great run fired us up the table and closed the gap on the top two. The goals were mainly coming from Gordon Dalziel, but he was helped by Ally Graham, Stevie Crawford, Danny Lennon and Colin Cameron pitching in on the scoring front.

As a defence, we were doing really well and had established a strong unit with excellent understanding. Most of the time, it was Steve McAnespie on the right, myself on the left, with Shaun Dennis, Davie Narey and Sinky in the middle.

Sometimes Jason Rowbotham and Ronnie Coyle would be drafted in if one of the other was suspended or injured. It was great bunch of guys to have alongside you in the heat of battle. We all knew how we worked and understood each other on the field. We had a cracking squad and nobody liked to be left out of the eleven, so the competition helped to keep you playing to a high standard.

As the games passed, we kept winning and were scoring freely. We were confident and we felt there was a chance of actually catching the top two. They must have been looking over the shoulders at us thinking 'these guys might actually catch us and deny us promotion'. Our goal was to keep winning to make them lose confidence to give us the upper hand. It worked a treat and going into the last few games we caught them both and slowly but surely reached the top of the league. We arrived at the last day of the season needing just one point for promotion and to secure an unprecedented league and cup double.

The last game was away against Hamilton Accies, who at the time happened to be ground sharing with Partick Thistle, so it was a return to my old stadium, Firhill. It was a lovely warm day, perfect for football, and we had fantastic support following us. The whole of the Jackie Husband stand on the far side of the ground was packed with Rovers supporters desperate for the club to gain promotion.

All we had to do was either win or draw and we would then be champions. By now, we were quite confident that we could do it. We had worked so hard to get back all the points required to take us to the top of the league, so there was no way we wanted to throw all that away by failing to do the business against Hamilton. I would have been devastated to lose it all now after such a long, hard fought season.

I already had a League Cup winners' medal, but I wanted the league champions' medal to go alongside it. The cup win had been brilliant, but we only had to win five games. The league was a full season of ups and downs and anybody that wins it, it is always richly deserved. We wanted it to be us, but we knew we need to be focused and on top form.

I wasn't aware of it at the time, but it was to be Gordon Dalziel's last game for Raith Rovers. Dazza had seen it all at the club and over the years had helped himself to a barrowload of goals across all the divisions. His goal scoring record was brilliant. He had seen the club rise from the old Second Division up to the Premier League to win their first ever major trophy.

He was one of the funniest lads you will ever meet with a quick minded sense of humour and he could destroy you in a moment with his humour. We had all been on the end of his quick wit, and although you did your best to give as good you got, Dazza always had the last word.

This would be his last word as a Rover's player. I'm sure he knew this at the time and was determined not to slip up at the final hurdle. I think the championship trophy was being held close by in Glasgow as we had the advantage and were favourites for the title. We just had to make sure that there would be no disasters and the trophy wasn't being whisked away elsewhere by 4.45pm.

We did our usual pre-match preparations and it was then time to go out and play the last game of that season. The game started well and, if I am honest, we were in total control. The only trouble was that we couldn't get the one goal we needed to finish them off. We had so many chances throughout the game but, unusually, Dazza and the other forwards couldn't find the net to relieve the pressure and tension amongst the players and the large Rovers support. I think if we had scored one then a few would have come, but it didn't happen.

As the game progressed, we were aware that one scary moment or mistake could end our promotion ambitions. As full-time approached it all got a bit tense, but finally the referee blew the final whistle and it was over. We were champions and were returning to the Premier League. We had done what people thought was impossible, and secured the double. When I left Firhill after struggling with a lack confidence, I would never had imagined that just a short time later I'd be back securing a League and Cup double for my new team. What an incredible season in football, the absolute high point of my career.

Being on that field after the game had finished was the best feeling. I felt more relaxed than the cup final and could enjoy it more. The fans there were enjoying the moment as much as we were, and we stayed on the park for a very long time so we could all enjoy the occasion together. I have a photograph from that day of myself and Davie Narey holding the First Division trophy up aloft together. Davie retired after that game so it would be one of the last photographs taken of Davie in football. What an absolute privilege to share that moment with a football legend. It was a very special afternoon for everyone associated with Raith Rovers.

Eventually, we left the field and returned to the dressing room. Just like after the cup final, the dressing room was full of all the staff, directors and playing staff that were not in the team on the day. There were lots of pats on the backs, hugs and handshakes and the champagne inevitably followed. We were getting used to champagne after matches! There were a few words said by Jimmy Nicholl and then it time to do some interviews and board the bus for Kirkcaldy. The trip back to Fife was just as special as the cup final bus journey. It would be another great night in the town, but as always, the combination of adrenaline and alcohol makes my exact memory of that night a little hazy.

I do remember during the summer months after the Hamilton game, that my Father came up to visit me. He was a very old man by then but he was very proud of what I had achieved that season. I took him to my sons' primary school in Dalgety Bay to show off the two trophies we had won. I picked up the trophies from Starks Park before the school event and then kept them at home the day after.

I had two of the most important trophies in Raith Rovers history in my possession at my home, and thought to myself, what if somebody finds out I have these trophies at my house and decides to steal them? I started to panic and decided that at night when I go to bed, the two trophies will be staying with me. And so that's what happened. Can you imagine, sleeping with the League Cup and the First Division trophy? The next morning, I quickly got them back to Kirkcaldy and into safe hands.

The one sad note at the end of a season is that players all go their own way for the summer. This would be the last time I shared a dressing room with Dazza, David Narey and a few of the other lads. When we returned after the summer, there were a few players that didn't come back for various reasons and there would be some new signings.

Things had moved on, but we had achieved so much together and it is a team that I will never forget. The bond we had as a team that season will always be special and to this day I know that I could phone up any of my old teammates and they would be there for me if I needed them, in the same way I would be there for them.

That unique bond was still there twenty years later when we all got together to celebrate the 20th anniversary of our cup win and that incredible season. I was invited back to Fife to be inducted into the Raith Rovers Hall of Fame as part of the cup winning squad. The Hall of Fame is a fantastic event that takes place every year at the Adam Theatre in Kirkcaldy.

It is put together by a great bunch of guys including Willie MacGregor, Alistair Cameron, Allan Crow, John Greer and the late Ally Gourlay. It is a wonderful event that celebrates everything that is great about Raith Rovers. This particular year, all the players that played in the 1994 Coca Cola League Cup final and the rest of the lads that played their part in the cup run were invited as special guests. We were joined by Charlie Nicholas and Jeff Stelling, who hosts Soccer Saturday on Sky Sports every Saturday.

The afternoon of the event we attended various events and then went to a bar that is owned by local businessman and Rover's fanatic Dennis O'Connell. A mix of players and fans enjoyed a great meal and we chatted about that great season. It was great to be back with the teammates that had achieved so much together. The League Cup trophy was there too so people could get their picture taken with it. The hours passed very quickly and I ended up sat at the bar with Gordon Dalziel, trying to educate each other on fine malt whiskies.

We were competing to see who knew the most and to be fair I think Dazza won, but then he is Scottish after all. You can imagine how things went as the bar staff kept lining up different whiskies with Dazza and I drinking each one put in front of us. By the time we had to leave to go to the Adam Theatre, we were a little tipsy to say the least.

We were brought onto the stage to the applause of the audience and to sit on sofas and then one-by-one we were interviewed by Bill Leckie, a really funny guy and St Mirren supporter. I was one of the last to be interviewed and started to get worried. All the other guys were telling all the stories about the time we played for Raith Rovers and I was left wondering what on earth is left for me to say! In the end, I had no reason to worry, as some more stories came to me, and the audience were laughing so I could relax.

During the evening, there were difficult and very emotional moments when the two guys that were no longer with us were honoured. The families of Ronnie Coyle and Ian Redford accepted their induction to the Hall of Fame and I think just about every person in the theatre had a tear in their eye at this point. I know I did as I thought about Ian and Ronnie, and how two wonderful footballers and men were no longer around to enjoy the moment.

The event could have gone on all night, but it finished and we all ended up back at the hotel drinking and reminiscing about our times at the club. It brought back some great memories of a special time at a very special club with some great teammates who I now consider friends for life.

Even as I write this, I am looking at the award we were given that night which has pride of place in my house. I even remember the small things like featuring in the Panini sticker book or being part of the football management computer games from that era. Young lads would come up to me in the street and tell me that I was in their team or they had just sold me to some other club. I now look back and think how lucky I was to have had that and I am truly grateful. Raith Rovers, particularly that 1994/95 season will always have a special place in my heart.

I look back on that season as the best of my career. It was a season that made all the struggles, setbacks and disappointments of my earlier career worthwhile. What a club, what memories, and there were more to come. We were back in the top flight and having won the League Cup, we had qualified for the UEFA Cup. Raith Rovers in Europe, what a thought.

Chapter Fourteen: The European Adventure

"Always remember that you are unique, just like everyone else"

I had just had the best season of my career, so I knew it would be hard to top. But I knew that there was a new experience waiting for me, playing in Europe. It was crazy to think that a small local club like Raith Rovers had qualified for Europe and might be taking their place alongside some of the giants of European football. But to do that, we know we needed to negotiate a few qualifying rounds first.

The draw for the first round landed us with a tie against Gotu Ittrotarfelag. Most of us couldn't even pronounce or spell it, never mind knowing anything about them as a team. It turned out they were from the Faroe Islands which was a tiny clump of rocks roughly halfway between Scotland and Iceland. The first leg was at home, so at least we had the chance to get off to a good start. There was a feeling and anticipation with the fans in Kirkcaldy at our first ever European match.

The game arrived and on a sunny evening we took to the field in front of a bigger than usual crowd. I felt ready and I wanted an early touch of the ball. Thankfully, I am involved a lot within the first few minutes and our team as a whole has have started well. You often get a sense at the start of a game how things are going to go, and it was clear from the opening exchanges that this evening is going to be a good game for us.

It doesn't take long before we are attacking on a regular basis and I cannot see how they can keep up with the speed and strength of our team. I think it showed that we play in a more professional country, and it gives the lads more and more confidence as we get closer to scoring that important first goal. The lads at the back know that it is vital that we keep a clean sheet. If the score over the two legs is level in European competition, then away goals count double so we know how important it is not to screw up and concede.

The game is going well and there's a great buzz in the stadium. I get the sense that Gotu know we are the stronger team and have come to defend and try and hit us on the break and perhaps escape with a lucky one goal win. However, we are dominating the game and knocking the ball about well and Gotu are struggling to compete. Twenty-one minutes into the game, Tony Rougier advances forward on the right and gets to the bye line. He looks up and puts the ball across the six-yard box where Jason Dair is waiting to slide in to score Raith Rover's first ever goal in European competition.

The goal was richly deserved and gave us even more confidence to try and get another quickly. This didn't happen, even though we had a few great chances and we head towards the dressing room at halftime with just the one goal lead.

The interval went by the usual way with a few drinks and listening to the gaffer hand out some advice to the team. I think he was happy with the way we were playing and just told us to keep going and we would get our reward. The rest of us would then talk to each other. I would usually chat away to Scott Thomson, as we normally sat next to each other in the dressing room. My main focus was always on resting, catching my breath and sometimes, getting a massage to the legs.

Within two minutes after the second half kicking off, Tony Rougier missed a decent chance with his head. However, shortly after, I got the ball on the left and took two players on, jinking in and out and then putting a deep cross over to the right. Tony was there to head the ball into the back of the net and we were two goals up. I was pleased with the assist and made my way back to our own half.

The game was flowing now and we were looking our usual self, playing the ball around and quick one twos and triangles. We knew that a third goal would probably be enough to see us through the tie so we pushed on in search of it. It came in the 77th minute, with a fantastic free kick by Steve McAnespie. Late in the game I managed to push forward and put in another lovely deep cross, which was met by Ally

Graham who knocked it down for Mickey Cameron to score the fourth.

The game ended and going back into the dressing room was brilliant feeling. We could never have dreamt of that result. What a fantastic game. It was even more of a wonderful night for me, as I was awarded man of the match. The return leg could not come quick enough for us, but we had to wait two weeks.

The return leg was on the 22nd August 1995. The main thing that comes to mind when I think about our first ever away trip in Europe is the flight to get there. Now I am not the best flyer in the world and things were made worse when we were told that there were only one or two pilots in Europe skilled enough to fly one of the larger aeroplanes into the airport at Torshavn.

Eventually, a pilot was found so at least we knew we could get there. To get onto the very short runway, the pilot has to drop the plane very quickly so that we don't fall off the end of the runway into the sea. This was all I could think about as we approached the last part of the descent. By the end of it, I was on the floor of the aeroplane and I wasn't the only one. Half of the team had joined me!

You cannot imagine the sudden drop in altitude and hitting the runway to get the brakes on quickly. It was a scary experience and not good for the heart before such an important game. I can still remember seeing the relief on the lads' faces when the plane finally came to a halt.

The game was played at Toftir Stadium which sat on top of a hill and the weather was atrocious. I felt for the small band of Rovers fans who had made the journey across to watch us. The match was tougher than expected and ended up being a hard fought 2 - 2 draw. Danny Lennon put us ahead in the first half. We played well and should have scored more than one. Gotu roared back at us in the second half and scored two goals that we really shouldn't have conceded. Stevie Crawford scored late on to make sure that we didn't lose the match and to send us through comfortably, 6 -2 on aggregate. It had been a horrible trip and the weather was awful, but at least the hundred plus fans that had travelled all the way, knew they had another European game to look forward to.

It was a lesson for us not to take opponents too lightly. I think maybe we went there expecting Gotu to roll over as they were four goals adrift, but they gave a good account of themselves especially in the second half and we should have known better to allow them back into the game. We were fortunate to have a comfortable first leg lead, so our slackness at the back wasn't punished. The manager let us know exactly how he felt after the game in the changing rooms.

All I had to worry about now was the flight home. The pilot had to get the plane off the tarmac and into the air very quickly, otherwise, a very large mountain was waiting for us. My tactic was to have several alcoholic drinks and try not to think about that mountain too much. It worked and we made it safely back to Scotland. Now we had to wait who we would get in the next round.

We had started the defence of the League Cup by beating Arbroath 2-1. The Premier League season had also started and although we lost our first two games, they were against the Old Firm so we weren't overly concerned. We had pushed Celtic all the way in the opening match of the season at Stark's Park, losing by just a single goal. The draw for the next round of the UEFA Cup paired us with Akranes of Iceland, a venue even further north than the Faroe Islands.

So much for the fan's dreams of travelling to somewhere hot on their European adventure! We knew this was going to be a tougher game than Gotu, but at least we were at home first, so could hopefully establish a good lead to take to Iceland. We always had confidence at home no matter who we played.

The preparations for the match were just the same as always. The banter, the music and the team talk by Jimmy Nicholl just before we went out. The game started well and the lads were zipping the ball around. This gave me confidence that we were going to get the goals we required tonight. The first ten minutes, Akranes hardly touched the ball. The only glimpse of any problems came once, when they showed their one touch triangle play, with their forward turning Shaun Dennis, but it came to nothing.

The move showed that they had ability though, especially the midfield and forward lads, so this wasn't going to be easy. As in the Gotu game, I had Tony Rougier playing in front of me at various times in the match. Having Tony in front always made life a little easier for me, and it helped me to get forward and put a few crosses in.

It wasn't long before our first goal came. Some great play on our right in the 14th minute involving three or four of our lads ended up just on the edge of their 18-yard box. Danny Lennon struck the ball towards the goal, and it took a very slight deflection. The goalkeeper was slightly obstructed and although he dived the right way, it went past him and into the net.

The crowd erupted, one-nil. What a brilliant start, and richly deserved. Now we had to push on and try and build up a good lead to take to Iceland. We continued to play well and we looked good for more goals, but although we were getting chances, we were hitting the woodwork or their keeper was stopping shots. We were comfortable and looking good and not unduly worried. Our confidence was misplaced as, just before half time, Akranes struck.

Some good passing play by them ended with Olafur Thordasson putting one past Tommo. To concede an away goal after playing so well was a blow and there was stunned silence around Stark's Park. We felt there was no way they deserved to be level after 45 minutes and the lads headed for the dressing room bitterly disappointed. We were frustrated as we felt we were by far the better team. We needed a lift up from Jimmy and Martin Harvey, and they gave us it, so we went out for the second half determined to put things right.

We started well and it only took until the 65th minute for us to get the second. Davie Kirkwood put a cross over and it was only half cleared and there was Danny Lennon to place the ball in the corner of the goals from sixteen yards. It gave us a further lift to try and get another. It arrived with only ten minutes of the match left when Micky Cameron set up Barry Wilson to roll the ball past the keeper. It had been a strong second half and, after the setback of conceding, we were delighted to have come away with a 3-1 win.

We had a two-goal lead to take to Iceland and we were confident that we could protect that. I felt we played really well on that night, and in my opinion, we should have been taking a bigger lead into the next leg, but it often doesn't work out like that when it comes to Raith Rovers. It's never that straight-forward. I looked forward to the trip to Iceland in a fortnight's time.

The first thing I remember about the return leg was staying at the Hotel in Reykjavik. The hotel had a roof that was covered in grass and various plants. The food on offer had everything you wanted, as long as it contained fish. There was fish for breakfast, fish for lunch and fish for the evening meal. On the plus side, at least we were allowed an Icelandic lager with each meal. We walked into the centre of Reykjavik and it was the coldest weather ever, even though it was only September.

It was no surprise that all the locals seemed to drive everywhere. We trained the day before the match at a local community football field and we were happy to get a sweat on quickly to save us from the cold. Training went well and we headed back to the hotel to rest for the game the next day.

The Akranes stadium was middle of nowhere, and again a small but vocal Rovers support turned up to cheer us on. The actual game was a strange one. I think Jimmy Nicholl was so keen to protect our two-goal lead that he panicked a little and decided to put a team out that had two sweepers, four defenders in front of them, three in midfield and one up front. This must have been the first Raith Rovers line-up in history with six defenders!

The game was tough. Akranes clearly fancied their chances and it was backs to the wall for most of the match. It was bad game with hard defending and having to soak up wave after wave of attack. We kept it goalless in the first half but when we conceded a goal, the pressure was really on. We knew that all Akranes had to do was find another and they would have progressed to the next round at our expense.

Even though another goal would mean the tie would finish level over the two legs, the goal conceded in Scotland would have been enough to knock us out on away goals. Thankfully, Scott Thomson had one of those days that 'keepers can have where they manage to keep everything out. He was brilliant, making save after save to keep the score at 1-0. The referee blew his whistle for full time, and we ran over to our travelling fans to enjoy the moment with them. We had won 3-2 on aggregate and were through to the next round. Our European adventure was set to last at least one more time.

My best memory of that day was back at the airport. We travelled back on the coach to the airport enjoying a beer or two on the way. By the time we arrived, the Raith fans were there and in the mood to celebrate. To make it even better, in walks my old St Mirren teammate, Gunni Thorfason. He was a native Icelander and was on his way for business somewhere. It was pure chance as he had no idea we would be there enjoying the beers and atmosphere with the fans.

It was like an impromptu Paisley reunion as our reserve 'keeper at the time was Les Fridge, who had also played at St Mirren with us and there was also journalist Chic Young, a well-known Saints fan. The plane was delayed and we had the best time drinking beer, chatting to my teammates past and present and mixing with the fans that had made the journey to support the team. We just didn't want that moment to stop. I could have honestly have stayed at that airport all night. What a day. We are in the next round, little Raith Rovers. This is what dreams are made of.

Chapter Fifteen: Playing the Mighty Bayern Munich

"In seeking happiness for others, you will find it yourself"

We couldn't wait for the draw as the chance of landing a big team were becoming greater. We finally got the one the manager, players and fans wanted. Bayern Munich. We were drawn away for the first leg, but the clubs decided to shift the tie around for television so Bayern travelled to Scotland first.

It was such a huge game that we had no option but to play the tie at Easter Road, the home of Hibernian Football Club in Edinburgh. It was a shame not to be able to bring the mighty Bayern Munich to Stark's Park, but we were in the capital city of Scotland and it seemed the perfect place to represent the country against the best football club in Germany and one of the best in Europe.

We stayed in a hotel just outside Edinburgh the night before the game. We set off for Easter Road and could see loads of Raith fans approaching the ground and showing their support. The lads and everyone on the coach were buzzing and you could just feel it was going to be an amazing night. As we arrived at the ground and went through the player's entrance there were hundreds of Raith fans waiting for us and offering their support.

Inside the dressing room, I sat there for a while reading the extra-large football programme. It was a huge glossy programme with a picture of the UEFA Cup on the front and there were even pages written in German for the Bayern Munich fans. You could tell even from the style of the programme that this was a huge game. Reading the programme brought home exactly what we were up against. The Bayern squad read like a who's who in football. Oliver Kahn, Thomas Helmer, Markus Babbel, Christian Ziege, Christian Nerlinger, Andreas Herzog, Mehmet Scholl, Jürgen Klinsmann, Dietmar Hamann and Jean Pierre Papin. That was just a few of the names at the club. Not a bad team there!

The game kicked off at 6pm, for television coverage I think. The early kick off was strange, but at least the fans could enjoy themselves even more after the match I thought. Jimmy Nicholl gave his usual team talk and we are ready to go out. We walk out through the Easter Road tunnel led by a piper and I am third in line. As usual, I am throwing up a football to help me keep calm.

I am now aware that I will be marking their winger, Alexander Zickler. This guy is a very tall, slim boy, who I learned from the programme had joined Bayern Munich from Dynamo Dresden and already had made over 60 appearances in the Bundesliga. I wondered if he knew who Julian Broddle was!

The game started and straight away we knew that this was at a completely different level to the previous

games against Gotu and Akranes. Bayern had most of the possession in the early stages and we were struggling to get a touch. We had barely had time to settle when, in the sixth minute, a ball was knocked over the top in between our central defenders. Scott Thomson advanced towards the ball but the pace of Klinsmann allowed him to nip in and lob the ball over Thommo and into the net. The German striker needed just one chance, and he took it. We were already a goal down. It was a bad start but we knew that we had to just stay in the game. Gradually we worked our way back into the game, with the young lads in our team starting to express themselves and show what they could do. We created one or two half chances, but reached the half still trailing to

Klinsmann's goal. We were proud that we had shown character after that early setback and managed not to concede again.

The second half started even better. We had some great chances and lots of the play, but just couldn't put that final finish to some wonderful play. I was getting a little more of the ball and getting forward for a change rather than having to defend for my life. Then suddenly, we had our best chance of the night. We won a free kick on the left just outside their box and I was the player to take it. I approached the ball slowly and looked up to see Mickey Cameron pointing to where he wanted the ball played quickly. The German defence wasn't ready so there was an opportunity to catch them sleeping. So, I fired the ball to where Mickey wanted it.

Fortunately for me, I whipped a precise cross into the 18-yard box just before the 6-yard box and Mickey rose up like a salmon and headed the ball towards the top corner of the net. The whole stadium, including me, waited for the ball to hit the back of the net. Frustratingly, Oliver Kahn pulled off an amazing one handed save to deny us the goal. That's why he played for Bayern Munich and would go on to feature for Germany in World Cup finals, becoming one of the world's top 'keepers.

If only we had scored, it would have given Bayern a fright and potentially lifted us up for a grandstand finish to the game. Instead, the German team maintained their one goal advantage and with 18 minutes to go, the lethal Klinsmann struck again and that was that. 2-0 to Bayern.

It was a disappointment to lose, but we realised that we had given a good account of ourselves and, but for the goalkeeping of Oliver Kahn and lethal finishing of Jurgen Klinsmann, it could have been a much tighter game. The fans appreciated our efforts and clapped us off the pitch. I often wondered afterwards if we had played them at a tight Starks Park, would we have done a little better and got that goal? Who knows, but it would have been nice to think of all those superstars cramped into the tiny away dressing room in Kirkcaldy preparing for the match. We had lost, but there was still the second leg to come. We would travel to the Olympic stadium in Munich needing to overturn a two-goal deficit. Easy!

We were due to play Bayern in Munich on the 31st October, Halloween night. This was a game that lots of Rovers fans didn't want to miss and around 1,500 made the journey from Fife to Germany to back the team. Let's be honest, there is very little chance that Raith Rovers will play Bayern Munich again in our lifetime in a competitive match, so it was a one-off opportunity for most supporters. The chance to play in the Olympic stadium was special, an arena that has seen so many triumphs and sadness over the years in both football and the Olympic Games.

We flew direct from Edinburgh to Munich and were then driven to the Sheraton Hotel, which I believe

Bayern Munich either owned or had shares in. Thommo and I roomed together as always and we settled in for the run-up to the game. That first night we knew we would be training on the pitch for about an hour at the Olympic Stadium. All the lads were excited about this and some had brought camcorders and digital cameras to take footage of the stadium while we were training.

We must have resembled a bunch of tourists on holiday at times rather than a football team about to take on Bayern Munich. Even the club directors came with us and I don't blame them as it's not very often you get the chance to look around such a magnificent stadium without thousands of supporters being there. We headed into the changing rooms and were stunned by their size. They were the size of a quarter of a football pitch and had a proper built in hairdryer for every player above where you changed. They must love their hair in Germany. If only I had access to that when I had my perm at Plymouth I thought.

So, we got changed and headed out onto the pitch. It was very eerie being at this incredible stadium at night with nobody in the stands. The training is light and enjoyable and it's over just as we are all getting into it, but it's necessary to be short as we don't want any injuries and we they don't want us damaging the pitch too much.

One of the lads, who shall remain nameless for obvious reasons, had brought a camcorder to capture the occasion. He asked John Valente to film us while we trained. John was our kit man and was a lovely man with a great smile. He would do anything for the club. He owned a fish and chip shop in Kirkcaldy and loved the club so much, that if you asked him for help with anything, he would try his hardest to help you. John brandished his usual smile and happily agreed to film the lads while we trained.

The footage would have been fantastic keepsake of a really special moment for the club, but incredibly the player in question discovered a porn channel on his hotel room TV that night and decided to record that. In doing so, he erased all the fantastic footage that John Valente had filmed at training earlier in the evening! Back at the hotel it was a quiet night and we have something to eat and then go back to our rooms to relax and to try and get some sleep.

The next day was just preparing for the match that night. I always tried to conserve my energy for the game. During the two days, we were at the hotel, I had got to know a couple of the staff. They were friendly, spoke English and it was always good to have some local knowledge. They wished us well and we boarded the coach for the drive to the stadium. We may have been off to face the German giants, Bayern Munich, but the banter and the music on the coach was the exact same as if we were heading to face Morton in the league.

As we got closer to the Olympic Stadium, we can see hundreds of Raith fans that had made the trip.

That gave us a boost, to think that people had come all the way from Fife to support us even though we trailed by two goals and faced a seemingly impossible task.

We arrived at the Stadium and walked inside to the huge away dressing room. John Valente and the young lads had already been in to set the kit and boots up and all we had to do was grab a programme for the collection. We walked out onto the pitch to have a look around and we could see the Bayern Munich and Raith Rovers supporters entering the ground early to soak up the atmosphere.

We returned to the dressing room and I got my number three shirt and kit on. It was my usual number and I very rarely played any other number in my time at Raith, unless I was a substitute and wore the number twelve. Kick-off approached and then it was time to walk out and prepare for one of the biggest games I would ever play in. Jimmy Nicholl had made Sinky the captain for the evening, which was a great honour, so he led the lads out and had to meet the referee and the opposing captain. Then it was game on.

We started well and, in my opinion, matched them in pace, passing and ability during that first 45 minutes. We had definitely improved from the first leg and were optimistic we could cause them problems. However, in the 22nd minute, disaster struck as

Ronnie Coyle brought down Christian Nerlinger in the box and the referee pointed to the penalty spot.

It was a blow, especially when we saw French striker Jean Pierre Papin stepping up to take the penalty. Incredibly, despite his experience and pedigree, he blasted it well over the top of Scott Thomson's crossbar!

What a relief and we felt we might still have a chance of doing something special. Bayern did have more play than us for the rest of the half, but that was to be expected. Their squad was packed with internationals and they were playing their 200th European game, while we had a mix of free transfers and youth players and were only on our sixth ever European match. We continued to compete and hope for a break.

That break arrived in the 40th minute. Mickey Cameron had been fouled on the left-hand side outside the 18-yard box. It was a difficult angle and a fair distance from the goal but Danny Lennon decided he would take the free kick. Directly in front of him was a Bayern Munich five-man wall. Danny approached the ball and curled it towards the goal. The ball took a slight deflection off the head of Herzog, which helped wrong foot Oliver Kahn in the Bayern goal and suddenly the net bulged.

Amazingly, we had scored. Bayern Munich- nil, Raith Rovers – one! The Munich crowd fell completely silent except for the Raith fans at the far end of the stadium that were suddenly going crazy. They deserved to as these moments usually only happen in dreams.

We returned to our own half and the game re-started. Bayern came at us but we survived comfortably to half-time. The boys got into the changing room quickly and sat down waiting for our Jimmy Nicholl to give his usual inspirational team talk. We all looked at him and he just burst out laughing.

Then we all started to laugh. The whole situation was ridiculous. We were leading Bayern Munich one-nil at in their backyard. We later found out that almost every Rovers fan there took a picture of the giant scoreboard showing the score line at half-time. As the laughter in our dressing room got a little quieter, the gaffer said 'listen', and we put our ears to the dividing wall to their changing room. All you could hear was their manager shouting at his team in German with the odd mention of 'Lennon', 'Dair', and 'Rougier'. We started to laugh again.

The halftime period passed quickly and it was time to go back out. As soon as the second half started, we had an amazing chance to score again. Tony Rougier blasted the ball wide from a cross, when with a bit more steadiness and nerve, he might have scored. It was a golden opportunity to level the tie. I could sense that after that chance they meant business. We were competing as best we could, but they were dominant and putting us under increasing pressure.

They finally got the breakthrough when Ronnie Coyle slipped and let in Zickler. He crossed to Klinsmann to score his fifth of the tournament. I felt for poor Ronnie. These things happen to all of us at some time in our careers and there's nothing you can do but take it on the chin.

Bayern stepped up another gear and although we had chances, it was inevitable that they scored a second. A corner in the 64th minute created a scramble in the six-yard box, and the ball was bundled over the goal line by Babbel. That was it, game over. We worked hard to get back into the tie but it wasn't to be. The final whistle blew and we had lost. I swapped my shirt with Zickler, and instead of walking off the pitch we all went across to our supporters to thank them for all the support during this incredible journey we had been on. I still have Zickler's strip at home and it something I treasure. I like to think that mine is a memory for him too, although I suspect he may have used at some point to wash his top of the range car!

Back in the dressing room there were several crates of German beer waiting for us. We left the stadium with several lads in one line holding the crates between them. I can still picture the scene now as we walked past some of the Bayern players still doing media interviews, with their opponents in the background carrying crates of beer. We headed back to the hotel before we got ready to go out into the city for a night out together with the supporters. We ended up in a German Beer Cellar with Scott Thomson and a few other players.

I was talking to some locals and some Raith supporters when I am approached by a German guy, who says there is a phone call for me. I take the call from a pay phone and it's the male and female staff from the hotel. They ask me to stay where I am and they are on their way down.

It was only after I put the phone down that I think how did they know where I am? If I didn't even know where I was! Twenty minutes or so later, they arrived and the party carried on, going on to other bars and having a fantastic night. By the time I get back to the hotel, it is the next morning and the coach is waiting to take us to the airport. The rest of the squad and staff and management are on it and I am told I have five minutes to get my things from my room or they are leaving without me. It isn't an idle threat, they would!

Fortunately, Scott Thomson had got my stuff ready for me, so it was just a case of running up to my room and picking up the bag.

The flight back to Edinburgh was great as there were lots of chat about the night before and a few more drinks to carry on the celebrations. The plane is on its descent when I hear a voice over the public announcer I recognise. It's Danny Lennon in the cockpit thanking us for flying with the airline and talking to us as if he was the captain. He later emerges the cockpit wearing the captain's hat.

Danny has been indulging on the way back and isn't exactly sober and as we enter the terminal there are several press people waiting for interviews. Poor old Danny has to talk to them, but thankfully he puts on a brilliant performance as if he had not touched a drop of alcohol in his life. You would never have guessed that he was still drunk!

So that's it, the incredible European journey is over and it's back to the Scottish Premier League. I would like to think that we did Scotland proud that year, and that our efforts will be talked about for many, many years around Kirkcaldy. It is great to go into Stark's Park today and see our achievement commemorated on one of the walls in the South Stand. I just smile when I look back at the footage now and think 'that was us, Raith Rovers, Simply the Best'.

Later that season we would lose the manager who had made it all happen. When I heard the news that Jimmy Nicholl had taken the Millwall job, I was devastated. We had lost our leader.

Jimmy was a fantastic coach. He knew how to get the best out of every single player and how to blend them into the strongest team possible. He took a mix of free transfers, young kids, and players at the other end of their careers and turned them into a team that feared no one. We all knew that we were not the best team in Scotland on an individual by individual basis, but we knew that we could compete with anybody. His communication skills and his enthusiasm just brought that team together. He got us to enjoy nights out, days out playing golf, taking the piss out of each other in the dressing room and just the banter. That togetherness was what got the team going and made us gel.

He we so enthusiastic about the training and would make it fun. I was never the best trainer at any time in my career, but you would come away from a Jimmy Nicholl training session having worked really hard but saying that I had enjoyed it. He had the ability to put across what he wanted us to do, and explain himself if you weren't quite getting what you were trying to do.

He just pulled all these different people and characters together and we just felt like one. I had never had that at any other club. Yes, we had banter at every club I was at and we had some good teams at Barnsley and Scunthorpe, but I never experienced that togetherness that we had at Raith Rovers. That togetherness was created by Jimmy Nicholl.

Everybody respected him.

I will always be grateful to him signing me and, once I had adapted to his way of thinking, making me an almost ever present in his team. He was always encouraging to me on a personal level. He never really gave me any stick or ripped into me in any way. I think he realised that with my character, and that when I wasn't playing well, I already knew when I was letting him down. He would just speak to me calmly and offer encouragement. He would say 'We need a bit more from your Brods. You can do it. You've got the engine of five players'.

When he left it was an enormous blow? The first few days after Jimmy Nicholl left were so strange. I felt numb. The training changed and all the old banter had gone. It was too serious and the atmosphere had disappeared. When Micky Cameron, Sinky and Stevie Crawford left to follow him to Millwall, we knew it was the beginning of the end. The team that had achieved so much was being broken up.

I don't blame the lads for going. It was a chance to get better wages and make it in England. In my opinion, they could have moved on to a bigger club that Millwall, especially Mickey Cameron, but they believed in Jimmy Nicholl as much as the rest of us did and the attraction of continuing their football journey with the gaffer would have been enticing.
I thought for a second, that he might have taken me to Millwall, but that wasn't to be. The rest of us were left on a sinking ship that gradually fell apart, as it didn't have that same feeling anymore.

I can't thank Jimmy Nicholl enough. Along with Allan Clarke, he was the biggest influence on my football career. He gave me the opportunity to play for Raith Rovers and experience one of the most successful periods in my football career and I will always thank him for that.

Chapter Sixteen:
Leaving Raith Rovers

"Life is a play that does not allow testing. So, sing, cry, dance, laugh and live intensely, before the curtain closes and the piece ends with no applause"

Jimmy Nicholl was going to be a hard act to follow for any new manager. He had taken the club to heights that they previously could only have dreamed off. However, we still had a very strong squad and a great team spirit. I was astounded when they announced that the youth coach Jimmy Thomson would the man to fill the position. It was a strange decision which left me and many of the lads puzzled. As a youth coach, Jimmy Thomson seemed average at best.

He had been there in the background but he never stood out as someone who could do a job for the first team. I couldn't treat Jimmy Thomson as a manager. He was the youth team coach and to go from that to suddenly, you are now the manager, a lot of the lads struggled with that. With the greatest respect to Jimmy, he wasn't held in that respect within the club.

He decided to surround himself with Jim McInally as assistant manager and Stevie Kirk as a coach. These two players were never part of the amazing times we had experienced during the Jimmy Nicholl era and I felt they lacked an understanding of what Raith Rovers were all about. They never tried to keep the spirit we had and never tried to understand the Raith Rovers fans. We had our way of doing things and I felt that if it's not broken then don't fix it. Why change what had made Raith Rovers work? They took over and decided very quickly to bring in players too quickly in my opinion.

I was part of the changes they had in mind. I had played every single game up to the middle of January that season, but they brought in a lad called Mark Humphries, who was given a chance to play in my place. I am sure this guy was a decent player, but he had no idea about what we were all about and during the short time I was there I don't think I heard him speak once. A far cry from the vocal characters we had at the club in the past.

I wasn't aware of it at the time but my very last game for Raith Rovers first team was away at Motherwell on 24th February, 1996. We lost one-nil and I was substituted in the 86th minute. My last ever first team match ended in farce as I was selected as the player to take the drugs test. I was so dehydrated that it took me ages to provide the sample, and by the time I had the team coach had left Fir Park without me. Luckily the referee lived in my direction and was able to drop me off on his way home.

After that match, I was basically bombed out of the squad and put in the reserves. The team I was in were the most successful team at Raith Rovers, and the seasons we had probably paid for the two new stands to be built. I didn't think you should treat players that were a big part of that success by kicking them in the reserves. I played a reserve game at Starks Park against Celtic reserves and I was told that I scored one of the best goals ever seen. I'd also thundered one against Pat Bonners bar that came out for Tony Rougier to score. That turned out to be my very last game in a Raith Rovers shirt.

It was a very sad way to end my career in Kirkcaldy. I still felt I could have contributed on the coaching side and helped keep the team spirit going that had been at the club for many years. In the end, all I received was a few words from Jimmy Thomson telling me East Fife wanted to sign me. I gave an interview to John Greechan, who was the reporter for the local press and also wrote a column in the programme.

He asked me how I felt about my time at Raith Rovers and how I felt now that it looked like my time was over. I told him that it was the most amazing time of my football career and that while players like me will come and go, the supporters will always be there for the club.

My Raith Rovers days were amongst the happiest of my football career. They provided me with lot of great memories, great friends and a couple of winner's medals which I am incredibly proud of. Every time I go back to Kirkcaldy, the people are always incredibly friendly and appreciative of the part I played in a fantastic period in the clubs' history. I was lucky enough to be a guest of the club at Kirkcaldy in 2016 when they played St Mirren.

It was great to be able to go into the home end before the game and meet the supporters. And to see the heroes of the 1994 cup final, including yours truly, commemorated with posters in that stand was humbling. I was asked to go onto the pitch at halftime to draw the raffle and do a very quick interview about my time at the club. It was fantastic to chat away and be allowed to say a proper thank you to Raith Rovers supporters, something I had been denied all those years before. I even walked to the away end to acknowledge the fans of St Mirren.

By the time I got home to England that night, my

social media had gone crazy with message and acknowledgements from both sets of fans. One fan, Chris Willett, even posted up a flag he had. It was a Scottish flag with the words 'JULIAN IS GOD, BRODDLE PURE GENIUS' emblazoned on it. I had never seen it before, but he told me that he had taken the flag to the cup final and all the way to Munich. I was totally blown away. To think that someone would actually take the time to put my name on a flag was a huge honour, especially given that I was from south of the border! I expressed my surprise and another Rovers fan, Don Manson, responded by saying that I underestimated my popularity and that I was still a hero to many of the Raith Rovers support. Another fan mentioned that I had the nickname 'scoop' amongst some of the support, something else I was totally unaware of. Apparently, it was based on the way I pinged the ball down the line.

I took it as a compliment and told them that I had been given a lot worse nicknames over the years. I felt humbled that fans who love their football team, appreciated the effort I put in and valued my contribution. I thank every one of them and will treasure the memories I have from the incredible Raith Rovers supporters.

Raith Rovers will always be the pinnacle of my football career. I had some fantastic times at a lot of football clubs, but nothing like the success we had in Kirkcaldy. It was just a fantastic time where everything we touched turned to gold. Raith Rovers is an era and a club that I will never forget. It is the one I cherish the most, the one I always go back to when I think about my football career, the one that I will always think 'they were the best days of my life'.

I joined East Fife with only six games left of the season. I didn't really want to leave Kirkcaldy, but I had learned throughout my career that when your manager doesn't want you then the best thing to do is move on to pastures new, preferably to someone who does want you.

The East Fife manager at the time was Steve Archibald, who I had played with in Paisley. The fact that they were only a few miles along the road from Kirkcaldy was an attraction and it meant that they were relatively close to where I lived. I was thinking of setting up a driving school, so I thought I could combine playing for the Methil club with establishing my business.

The training at East Fife was good when we all got together, however, 99% of the lads were part time and we only trained twice a week in the evenings. There isn't much to say regard my playing time at the club, other than we didn't lose any of the six games I played in, and we gained promotion out of the bottom tier of Scottish football. I celebrated with the lads obviously, but I didn't really feel part of it if I'm being honest. I was still dwelling on what had happened at Raith Rovers and was thinking ahead to what I was going to do next. I had qualified as a driving instructor, so I was thinking about doing that and staying part-time.

I used to get my wages direct from Steve Archibald. He handed them to me personally, so I suspect that he was paying my wages out of his own pocket. I had no evidence of that, but he was a wealthy man from his time in Spain and I had a gut feel. He was a good manager and I never understood why he didn't go onto better things in the game. I think he does a lot of Spanish TV now as he's fluent in the language, so I suppose he doesn't need the hassles of football management.

After the short period at East Fife, I was considering my options during the close season. I got a call from Ross County to see if I fancied a move up there. As I hadn't heard from Steve on a contract at East Fife, I decided to take a trip to north to speak with their new manager, Neale Cooper.

When I arrived at the club and met Neale Cooper and the Chairman, I felt that this was a club with potential. It's in a beautiful area of Scotland and they had a nice, compact football ground. I was aware the Chairman was quite wealthy and had big ambitions for the club. I had the meetings in a beautiful local hotel and agreed to join. No sooner had I made the commitment, my phone rang and it was Steve Archibald asking if I was prepared to sign a new contract with East Fife.

Talk about bad timing! I told Steve where I was and that I had just agreed to sign for Ross County only minutes before his call. He immediately said that East Fife would match the same deal as Ross County. This put me in a tricky position. I really liked Steve, and East Fife was closer to home, but I had just shaken hands with Neale Cooper on a deal and

I felt Ross County had more potential than the Fife side. If Steve had called me 24 hours earlier, then I probably would have signed on again for East Fife.

Over time, it was a decision that both I and Neale Cooper probably came to regret, but for now I had made my choice and prepared for life at Ross County. I had gone part-time and trained twice a week at either Raith Rovers or Dunfermline as both were close to where I lived. A lot of Ross County players lived in Glasgow and Edinburgh area so I would meet up with other lads in Perth, and we travelled up together in rented vehicles. The banter was great and the time would pass quickly.

The main problem I was experiencing was that because I had gone part-time, my body decided it would fall to bits! I put some weight on and every time I trained I felt slow and unfit. It became clear fairly quickly that part-time football didn't suit me but the decision had been made and I would just have to get used to it.

We got through pre-season and then the competitive games started. Almost straight away, Neal Cooper and I were not getting on and I was struggling with my game. There were some cracking footballers at Ross County and they were expected to get promotion, but the as the season progressed it was clear they were quite unpredictable. I was struggling.

I played well twenty minutes here and there or even the odd half, but my confidence was low and I was inconsistent. Neal Cooper was new as a manager and didn't know where to play me or how to get the best out of me and I don't think he was ever happy with my game. I could sense over time that he didn't like me, and this only made things worse. The season slipped by and most games were forgettable. There were only the odd games that stood out and they tended to be for the wrong reasons.

I can remember playing Queen's Park in the League Cup at Hampden Park, the Scottish national stadium. It was where we should have played the match against Celtic in 1994 if it hadn't been undergoing renovation at the time. We lost and as I walked off the pitch, I was grabbed by the match sponsors as they thought I was man of the match. I knew I hadn't played well was embarrassed having my photos taken with the sponsors in front of a brand-new mountain bike, which was the reward for being man of the match. I walked into the changing room with my brand-new bike just as the manager was ripping into the lads for the performance. When he looked around and saw me with this gleaming bike, I could only imagine what he was thinking.

That night I was travelling up to Inverness to collect a brand-new car that was part of my contract. I had arranged to pick it up and drive back down to Fife. I put my new bike in the boot of the bus and then got on the bus and sat down with the boys who lived up north.

During the trip north, the manager was sat near the front and I was at the back. It was a long journey but as we got near to Inverness, I walked up to the front of the coach and spoke to the driver to ask him to drop me off in town somewhere. A minute or two before the coach pulled up, Neal Cooper asked me why I was being dropped off in Inverness. I told him that part of my contract was a brand-new car and I had arranged to pick it up that night. His face was a picture. We had just been knocked out of the cup and here I was with my brand-new bicycle and picking up a brand-new car. I think he was fuming inside.

The season passed and I played the odd game, but before long Cooper wasn't picking me. We lost out on promotion to our fierce rivals, Inverness Caledonian Thistle. The following season continued in the same vein. I would get the odd game until I was told not to bother travelling anymore. They effectively told me to stay at home unless I was required for the reserve team. My last game for County was in 1998. It was an away match against Inverness Caledonian Thistle and we got stuffed.

As I drove away from the ground by myself, I was very down about the game and my own performance. It turned out that this would be my last ever professional game as not long after Ross County paid me off and that was that. My career which started in 1981 at Sheffield United had finished in 1998 in Inverness. I had enjoyed 17 years as a professional footballer and experienced high and lows in equal measure. Up until that point I had known only football, but it was now time to begin the next phase of my life and look for a new challenge.

Chapter Seventeen: Life After Football

"Do not regret growing older. It is a privilege denied to many"

Leaving football wasn't easy. Trying to get my head around everything was difficult. I struggled a lot and it was quite a dark time. If you come out of football after never having done anything else your whole adult life, then you don't know what the real world is like out there. You have spent most of your life working for two or three hours a day and then kicking a ball about for 90 minutes on a Tuesday or a Saturday.

Then you have the fantastic nights out and, even though I had never hit the heights in my career, the modest celebrity that comes with along with playing football. Once I had left the game all that disappeared. I was on my own, probably for the first time in my life.

I wasn't sure what to do next, so I decided to concentrate on my driving instruction full-time. On paper, it was a great idea, but the reality was harder to adjust too. The hours were very long and when you are driving around the same area again and again it starts to become very boring very fast.

I enjoyed meeting people and it was good to know that you had helped someone pass their driving test, but I was struggling with it. I was working constantly and I was shattered. I was trying to be so nice and enthusiastic for everybody who I was teaching to drive. You would try and get Sunday off, but then people would phone up and say it's the only day I can do it. So, the next thing I knew I was working eight to ten hours on a Sunday as well.

My driving test centre was in Dunfermline, so no one really made a big deal of me having been a footballer. Most of my clients were females so it was never really an issue. I was teaching a lot of young female school kids to drive and they would recommend them to their friends, so I spent a lot of time parked up outside the local high school waiting for them to finish school. The only embarrassing moment of being recognised was actually nothing to do with football.

I had recently had a vasectomy in the local hospital and a few weeks later I was driving past the hospital with an older woman learner. As part of the usual banter, I told her that I'd recently been in there and what it was for. She looked a bit sheepish before replying, 'Well my daughter told me not to tell you, but I was your nurse and I was the one holding your hand while you had it done!'

The main downside of the job was that I was sitting in a car all day. I wasn't moving around so I started to put on weight on. I was still eating the same sort of food and drinking the same as I always had, but I wasn't running it off at training. I realised that I would probably never be fit again.

It was around this time that I was having a lot of problems in my personal life. My marriage to Jan was in a bad way. I was working long hours so I was never home and I wasn't seeing the kids as much as I wanted. That left Jan to cope alone. The final breakdown in any relationship is a difficult thing to talk about, especially without the permission of the other person involved.

We struggled along for about 18 months until Jan left me taking our three young children with her. She took the kids back to Liverpool and I was left in Scotland, alone and in an empty house.

Jan had been with me all the way through my football career and moved from place to place as I moved clubs. At the time, I never thought much about Jan having to keep moving around with me, it was just what we did. She would get jobs in the civil service and get settled and then I would be changing clubs and she would have to leave and start all over again in a new job, with new people and a new area. It never crossed my mind to ask her if she was ok with moving to the next club and then to the next club. I just took it for granted that she would just go along with it.

We never had grandparents living close by ever so the bulk of the job of bringing up the kids fell on her shoulders. I helped with night feeds and changing nappies when the kids were babies, but looking after three children is an exhausting job and she did it without complaining. She would often go to her parents in Liverpool for a much-needed rest. When I first moved to Plymouth Argyle, our son was a baby, she would send me video tapes of him, with Jan pretending to talk for him.

The tapes were a great comfort for me, as babies change so quickly, and I didn't want to miss out on anything.

Jan did what she needed to do to get by and support out family. She once got herself a job painting thousands of bear figurines as she could do it from home and fit it around looking after the children. As I worked relatively short hours I would often help her. When I retired from football, Jan worked part-time as a call taker at the Sky complex in Dunfermline.

The job was nightshift so I had to look after the kids, but it wasn't too hard as most of the time they were asleep anyway. Jan would get home in the early hours of the morning and be shattered. She eventually got a job as cabin crew staff with British Caledonian, not long before our marriage broke down. It was a huge blow. Whatever happened between us, Jan was a fantastic mother to our children, and raised them in the right manner.

We were married for thirteen years and had a lot of happy times together. If it was a different era, then she could have enjoyed the lavish lifestyle that football now offers players and their spouses, but we did our best and hopefully she has many good memories as the wife of a journeyman footballer.

It wasn't long before I realised that things had to change. I was living alone in an empty house, I hated my job and I was depressed. It was a dark time.

I decided to leave Scotland, so put the house up for sale and started making plans to move back to South Yorkshire. The house sold in one day and, after eight years living in Scotland, I moved back to my home village of Laughton. As the weeks went by, it became clear Jan and I weren't going to get back together and divorce proceedings began. It was time to look for something new to do with my life.

Chapter Eighteen: The Police

"Sometimes life will test you but remember this, when you walk up a mountain, your legs get strong"

When I arrived back home, I had to sign on for the first time in my life. I had thought about joining Worksop Town. They were part-time and were in the Northern Premier League, but I just wasn't fit. I just couldn't handle the pace and my legs had gone. Everything was sore and I knew that was the end of my football career.

It was then that I decided to try and join the Police. It was something that my Dad had experienced and I thought, if he had still been around, then he would have been very proud of that decision. I started training and running to try and get fitter and took a course at a college in Rotherham that helped in entering public services like the fire service or police service. I was still struggling with the breakdown of my marriage and the fact that my three children were over 100 miles away. Applying for the police force became a welcome distraction.

I knew that most forces accepted multi-applications, but for some reason South Yorkshire didn't accept people applying to other forces. I couldn't take the chance of having only one opportunity to get through, so I turned them down and applied to number of different forces. I was eventually accepted by Greater Manchester Police. I moved to Buxton which was close to where I would be stationed in the Stockport Division. By then, I had

 started a new relationship with Sarah Beattie, a woman from my village who was eight years younger than me and a keen Sheffield United fan. I had met up with my old school mates and we had gone out in Rotherham. The drinks had flowed and we ended up in a nightclub. It had been years since I had been to a club but I met Sarah and we swapped mobile numbers. A few days later we had our first date and soon became an item. When I was accepted into the police, Sarah decided move to Buxton with me.

Working in the police reminded me a lot of being a football player. You had that bond and trust that came from being part of a team. There was the banter and your team would do anything for you. You would often find yourself in really difficult situations at times and you had to rely on each other 100%. I loved that sense of togetherness. The main difference was that there were now females in your team. Working in football, you never had to work with females, so that was a different mindset, but it was easy to adapt to as everyone was working towards the same goal.

When you first go out on the beat you haven't got a clue what you are doing. They can train you all day long at the college and even though you supposed to know what you are doing, when you step out onto the beat for the first time, you are just a nervous wreck. In a sense, it was no different to walking onto a football pitch as a 16-year-old to make your debut for Sheffield United. I was lucky in that I was slightly older. I have since tutored a lot of young cops in their early twenties.

If you have to go out to a domestic between two fifty-year olds and you have this 22-year-old cop trying to tell them what to do, it is not realistic. I think it takes about five or six years until you have seen it all and done it all and truly know what you are doing. I think only then can you have the authority that you need to do the job well.

Stockport was then split into four sub divisions, and I was placed at Hazel Grove Police Station, off the A6 heading out towards Derbyshire and Cheshire. It was a great area to work. Although it had some difficult areas, the patch consisted of mainly nice areas. The shifts were hard to get use to at first, as they included night shifts, but I loved every minute of my new job and team. Because I was older, I was out through the driving course and allowed to drive Police cars, Police vans and 4x4 vehicles.

My police training came in handy on a day off from work in 2001. I went to visit my kids in Liverpool and took them to their horse riding lessons at Croxteth Park. I would pick them up at Jan's home and watch them ride. On this particular occasion, Jan decided to come with us and after dropping the girls off, we went for a drive around the park as the girls were heading off on a cross country trek. As we were driving around the park, a young girl came running out of the tree line and almost landed on our car bonnet.

She was only about 13 or 14 years old and was clearly traumatised. I quickly slammed the brakes on and the girl and jumped out of the car to discover what was wrong. She was screaming that her friend was drowning in the park river. We ran to the very steep bank and got into the water, where the young girl was unconscious under the flowing river. We got her head out of the water but then tried not to move her just in case of any spinal injuries. We called 999 and explained the situation.

Jan and I then took it in turns to do mouth to mouth on the girl, and eventually she let out a huge gasp and water poured out of her mouth. She became hysterical but we tried to calm her down and keep her as steady as possible.

We kept talking to her, trying to keep her awake as we waited for the Ambulance. It finally arrived about 40 minutes later and when they saw where we were, they initially didn't seem too keen to get in the water. I was getting angry with them and told them to get down and help us as she was far too heavy to get up the bank by ourselves. They checked her out and slowly got her out of the water and into the Ambulance. They took our details and that was that. When I got home that night I didn't mention the incident to Sarah. She could be a very jealous person, so I didn't want to get into an explanation about why I was driving around a park with my ex-wife. I went straight upstairs when I got home and changed out of my wet clothes.

A few months later I got a call to see Chief Inspector Hull. He told me I would receive several awards for saving the girl's life and that some newspapers had been in touch and wanted to do an interview. I was initially reluctant, as it would mean having to tell Sarah, but he said it would be good publicity for our division and would help me through my Police probation period. In the end, I had no choice. I went home and told Sarah about what had happened and what was going on. As expected, she was furious. Greater Manchester Police had organised for Jan and I to meet the girl in Stockport Police Station with the media present.

I found out her name was Rebecca Marsden, a 14-year-old from Liverpool. Her mum told me that while Rebecca was in hospital, she had four brain bleeds and almost died, but had gone on to make a full recovery. It was lovely to see the young lady, looking well and happy. She told me that she and the other girl had been swinging on a rope across the river bank, when the rope snapped. Rebecca had fallen into the river banging her head on a rock, knocking her out. After hearing her story, I was just happy to be in the right place at the right time.

Sarah was feeling homesick so I transferred to a station in Ollerton with Nottinghamshire Police. I was sad to leave my colleagues and the new job was very different. I had gone from having police officers everywhere near me, to just a few covering a vast area. I was missing Manchester and I'm pretty sure I would have frustrated my new colleagues talking about Greater Manchester Police all the time. It was hard to adjust to dealing with local issues and not the sharp end of Police work. A lot of my time was taken up with bike thefts and disputes between neighbour. An indication of the pedestrian pace of the area was that one of the highlights was attending

Sherwood Forest to investigate report of people dogging.

I used to love creeping up on them late at night, then switching on the Police sirens and lights to give them a fright. It was amazing how quickly all the parked cars would disappear when a Police vehicle arrived. I quickly transferred to a similar place called Carlton in Lindrick to be closer to home. I thought if I had to do this kind of police work, then I might as well do it close to home so I didn't have far to travel. I worked there for about one year, and although it wasn't what I wanted, I kept my head down and got on with it.

After five years of a relationship with Sarah, we broke up. She had been the reason for leaving Manchester, so I quickly set the ball in motion to return to Greater Manchester Police. I moved back to my old station, Hazel Grove, but in a different team this time. One of my old mates from previous group, Gareth Meadows, was my Sergeant, which was a bonus we had a strong bond from the past. The team had been through a tough time recently as an undercover reporter from the Daily Mail had joined the team to investigate racism in the police. He had hidden cameras and microphones on the whole time and later produced a documentary with the hours of footage. Some of it was shocking, but the worst footage was from his training in Warrington and involved officers from Wales, not from Greater Manchester Police. A few Manchester Cops were suspended and as a result we needed new officers. I was asked to tutor the new officers that were coming in. Morale after the incident was very low and officers were suspicious of any new recruits coming in.

I remember one colleague I tutored called Jim Wilson, who was very well educated and a really nice guy. On his very first day on shift we were called to deal with a sudden death. The deceased had taken his own life by using a hose from the exhaust pipe of his car run into the interior. Even though it was his first day, Jim was calm and confident and dealt with the situation so well. Another death we were called to was an elderly lady who had passed away in her bathroom.

She had been left there for several days with the heating on and as soon as we opened the letterbox, the smell just hit you. I was the tutor and Jim was the probationer so I used my authority and told Jim to go in first. He had to smash the glass pane in the front door then crawl in through the door. Welcome to the force Jim. We had a cracking team and a good spirit and there were quite a few enjoyable nights out in Manchester with my colleagues.

By now, I was living with my new partner, Julie. At that time of life, Julie was perfect for me. She was a lovely person and very spiritual. She introduced me to walking and we spent many happy days walking in the Lake District, Snowdon, Derbyshire and Scotland. I even did a week walking in the French and Italian Alps, finishing with Mont Blanc. We got married at Gretna Green in 2005 and lived in Warrington, Cheshire. At first, the simple life was what I needed. We were going to invest in a property in the Lake District, as Julie had good friends that had a hotel in Coniston.

The idea was that it would be a kind of pension plan. All was going well with the purchase, right up to doing the survey and purchasing furniture for the place. We even had struck a deal with a company to help us advertise the cottage to tourist. Then it just hit me. I thought 'I cannot do this'. I didn't want to commit to the rest of my life living in Warrington and having the pressure of looking after a cottage many miles away. I knew I had to tell Julie and I knew it would devastate her.

Around that time, I had got back in touch with someone I knew from high school. Jane Szekeres was three years younger and had been someone I was aware of, although Jane will say that I was more interested in her friend at school. When I left to play football, our lives went their separate ways. It wasn't until 2002 that I saw her again in a local pub. She was there with her friends and boyfriend. Jane is the life and soul whenever she is out with friends, and I could see her dancing, singing and loving her night out. I had the feeling that one day we would get together even though at the time, I couldn't say how.

We had become friends on Facebook and I would comment on her status or like her photographs. I eventually messaged her and we immediately clicked. We were both married, but we enjoyed our friendship and it wasn't long before we exchanged phone numbers. Eventually, we agreed to meet up on the Woodhead Pass, at the Dog and Partridge pub. I was nervous at first, but as we started to chat it was great and when we got back into our cars to head home.

Not long after leaving I called her on my car phone, and told her I had forgotten to give her a present for her birthday. Jane later told me if I hadn't have called her so soon she would have thought our meet up was a failure. From that point on we would make any excuse to meet up or call.

We both knew it was wrong as we were married, but sometimes you cannot help falling in love when you meet the right person and Jane was that person. Eventually, I left Julie to be with Jane. Julie had been a very positive influence on my life the seven years we had been together. She was someone who loved everything she had at the time and lived life to the full. She soaked up everything that was good like a sponge and I believe to this day, she continues to practice Spiritualism and Reiki. I regret any hurt I caused her and I truly hope that she is happy and well.

Jane and I have been together now for several years and live in Dinnington, back in the area where we both grew up. It has been a fantastic time and we have had some amazing experiences. We just click in every way. Things have not always been easy for

Jane in the time we have been together. In 2015, Jane was having some pain in her stomach area, and went for several tests at the local surgery. She was sent to Sheffield for further tests where it came

to light that she had Polycystic Kidney disease (PKD). PKD is a disease where, as you age, cysts start to grow on the kidneys and by the time you are in your mid-fifties the kidneys will fail.

We now go to regular appointments to see how Jane's kidneys are doing and to try to control the situation. Unless she can find a donor then she will be on dialysis for the rest of her life or worse.

The one positive of the situation is that she had to contact people in her family so that they could get tested. At the time, Jane had not spoken to her brother Paul for 23 years as they had fallen out over something and nothing in the past, but Paul needed to be told so he had the choice to have himself checked out. We decided that I should go and visit Paul to let him know. I was obviously a complete stranger to Paul and his wife Karen, but I knocked on their door and they were very nice to me as I explained the situation. Amazingly, the very next day Jane received a text from Paul saying he was sorry that she had PKD and that he would get checked out. It was their first contact in over two decades. The conversation continued and they eventually met up and reconciled their differences - the only good news coming from this awful illness. Thankfully Paul, Jane's mum Ann and her two children were given the all clear and it appears that Jane is the first to carry the illness in her immediate family. When the time comes for Jane, hopefully she can find a match to replace her kidney. I have told her that I am prepared to donate my own kidney either for her or other people in her situation if ours don't match. Hopefully, some people reading this would think about doing the same to make life easier for those suffering from PKD.

I continued to work away in the Police and loved every minute of it. Occasionally, my football past would catch up with me. I often worked at football matches and once in Bolton I asked to stand and make sure no one approached the Norwich City coach as it arrived. I felt a bit awkward about it as the manager of Norwich was Paul Lambert, who I had played with at St Mirren.

It just brought home to me the extremes of life. We had been colleagues' years before in Paisley and there he was a Premiership manager, probably on a million-pound wage and there was me as a police officer earning a reasonable, but modest salary and stood outside his coach protecting him just in case any crazy Bolton Wanderers fan decided to have a go.

My Raith Rovers past also helped at times. One-year Labour had their conference at Manchester and all the top politicians were there including Tony Blair and Bill Clinton. They all had their special security so

we were just there as back up on both ends of their floor. We just had to watch the doors and not let anybody through. It was an easy shift which mostly consisted of sitting there reading the newspaper. The word got around that I was an ex-footballer and had played for Raith Rovers, the team that

Chancellor Gordon Brown supported. So, they brought him over to meet me and I was talking to him for ages. I asked him if he had gone to the League Cup Final and he told me he couldn't as he was busy at the time. I asked if he'd been in Munich and he told me the same.

I joked with him that he wasn't much of a Rovers' supporter if he'd missed the two biggest games in their history. He took it in good spirit. My Sergeant at the time was hovering in the background and I think his nose was put out of joint that I was having a laugh and a joke with Gordon Brown, so he moved me down to the foyer which was far removed from where the main politicians were. I'm at my new position in the foyer for only ten minutes and suddenly all these security guards appear and there is former US President Bill Clinton.

He comes straight towards me, says hello and starts chatting, asking me how British Police officers cope without guns and other questions. My next break, I took great delight in thanking my Sergeant for moving me as I'd got to meet Bill Clinton and was talking to him for ages. He was furious!

There were also extremely challenging times working in the police. I was on patrol in Bolton in May 2008. It had been an unremarkable night and I was on single patrol. Around 4am, I decided to drive down to an area called Stoneclough, which was part of my patch. On my journey, I noticed two males running out of a side alleyway which I thought this was strange.

I quickly turned my car around, just in time to see the two males enter a car and set off in the original direction I had been heading. I turned my car around again and set off to follow them. The car in front was travelling a normal speed so I used my personal radio to do a routine vehicle check. I shouted the vehicle registration and awaited a reply. The problem with the area I was in is that it is bad for communication and the control room were struggling to hear my call.

I repeated my message but again, no response. After a third try, I thought it best just to pull the car over to check the two males out. I lit up my emergency lights and the car indicated to show it was pulling over. I felt quite safe as they not tried to get away and they had been keeping to the speed limit. The surrounding area was deserted but I felt confident that the call takers in our control room knew where I was as technology inside my personal radio let them know my location.

I pulled in ten metres behind their car, got out of my car, locked it and started to walk towards their vehicle. Suddenly, three masked up males jumped out of their car and rushed towards me. I had seconds to make a decision as I could see they had sledgehammers and what looked like a shotgun. I sprinted back to my car, got in and tried to use my emergency button to alert the control room.

At the same time, I was trying to start the car to get out of there. One of the males immediately jumped onto my car bonnet and started to smash the windscreen with his sledgehammer. Another was using a hammer to smash the front passenger window. The third smashed my front driver's side window and pointed the shotgun at me,

'Give me your fucking keys or I will blow your fucking head off'

The second male is leaning through the passenger side trying to grab my personal radio off my body armour, but he can't get it loose. The splinters from the front windscreen being smashed are cutting into my skin. The guy with the gun repeats his threat, telling me to keep my head down and stop me looking at him. By the time he starts to say it for the third time, I have already thrown the car keys to the ground at his feet. I had my head down but I suspect he grabbed them as they all rush back to their car.

I can already hear police sirens in the distant as they speed off in their car. I am in shock, but I can hear the control room asking if I am alive. They had heard the commotion on the radio followed by silence as gathered my composure. I then let them know I am ok. My white shirt is covered in blood but I have no real injuries to mention. My colleagues arrive on the scene and I am trying to tell them what has just happened, but I feel I am in a world of my own, almost as if everything is in slow motion. It's hard to describe the emotions I was experiencing. I'm soon sat on the roadside looking back at the surreal sight of my smashed-up patrol car.

It's not long before high-ranking officers arrive, as they always do at serious incidents, and I am taken to one side by some Commander. He asks me if I am ok and then who I am and where I have worked, possibly to distract me and help me calm down. When I tell him, I was involved in another firearms incident earlier in my career, he laughs and tells me to remind him never to work with me as wherever I go, somebody pulls out a gun!

Eventually, I get back to our Station and hand in my uniform as it is needed for any forensics. They insist on driving me home as I might still be in shock. As soon as I am left alone, I sneak out, get in my car, and drive away quickly. At the time, I felt I just needed to get anyway and gather my thoughts. By the time I get home, I am getting messages from my colleagues asking if I am alright, with some joking that I could get a few months off work with stress after this. I finally get into bed and just lay there, replaying the incident over and over again in my head, reflecting on how lucky I had been.

One of the worst days of my police career was 18th September 2012 when we lost my colleague Fiona Bone and Nicola Hughes when they were cruelly murdered by Dale Cregan. I had transferred to Ashton under Lyne Police Station and the day started normally. There had been ongoing enquiries to locate Cregan, as he was wanted for murder, but there had been no sign of him so we assumed he was being hidden by associates.

I was working with a colleague and good friend Peter Reed. Pete and I were doing normal work, when all of a sudden; there was an alarming call on our personal radios that there had been gunshots and officers down. We sped off to assist and it wasn't long before we got to an area called Hyde and located the road to be confronted with our worst nightmare.

We were one of the first patrol cars to arrive at the scene, but the paramedics were already there and working on Nicola and Fiona, trying to keep them alive. We were soon joined by numerous patrol cars and in a very short period of time, firearm officers and CID officers gathered. I overheard one of the senior paramedic officers say that one of the officers hadn't made it, and even though they were still working on the other officer, it's highly unlikely she will survive. The police force is one big family, and we all go through the pain when we hear such words. It was a devastating blow.

Orders were given to clear the area, but I thought 'I'm going nowhere', so offered to start the door to door enquiries. I felt that I had to do something. The senior officer agreed, and so off I went knocking on doors and getting any details, I could to help our enquiries. I could already see the stress and horror on the faces of my colleagues who were leaving the scene.

The neighbours had heard bangs and some had said they saw hand grenades being thrown at the girls' police van. I passed on the information to the senior investigating officer. I cannot imagine what he was thinking, but he must have been under incredible pressure. I drove back to Ashton under Lyne Police Station. It wasn't long before colleagues came over to me and asked what was going on. I told them that the officers were dead and there was shock.

I went upstairs and there was a team ready to inform every one of the situation. As I opened the door, I saw our Chief Superintendent, the entire team that worked with Fiona and Nicola, and several other supervisors. There was total silence in the room. The Chief Superintendent and the Deputy Chief Constable were stood together waiting to tell us what they knew and what was currently happening Neither mentioned the situation of Fiona and Nicola.

Suddenly, one of the constables shouted, 'Sir, how are Nicola and Fiona? Are they going to be alright?'

Wow, they didn't know.

The Chief Superintendent told them calmly that Nicola and Fiona were dead. You can imagine what happened next, and even I was close to tears. We were told that if we wanted counselling then it would be there for us. The shift ended and many of us went to the local pub to try to make sense of the events of the day. As we sat trying to come to terms with what had happened, one of my colleagues suddenly remembered that Nicola and Fiona just handed in their deposits for the Christmas party. The team had just agreed a venue that morning and everyone had been really excited for the Christmas get together.

The two women hadn't even meant to be working together that morning, but had asked if they could as they had stuff to discuss, including the Christmas function. They were tasked to go to a suspected burglary and had their lives taken away from them when Cregan shot them in cold blood. He then drove away at speed and later handed himself in at Hyde Police Station, allegedly saying he was sorry it was two female officers he had killed.

The following weeks were surreal. There were police officers from all over the Greater Manchester area and beyond wanting to help out on their days off. Messages came pouring in from the UK and across the world. I just hope in the tragic deaths of Nicola and Fiona that the public recognise what dangers the police face every day.

If the public could actually spend time on the front line, then perhaps they will understand what officers have to face and how, in recent years, we have been struggling to cope. Police budgets have been stripped by the Government and thousands of officers and staff are leaving the force.

They might be retiring, pensioned off or simply cannot take the pressure any longer, but that is making it harder and harder for the officers left to do their job. I was very proud to have been a cop and I think it is important to remember that when people are running away from an incident, it is the police and the other emergency services that are running towards it.

The police sometimes get the blame for things that are wrong in society. I know that there are some bad apples, there are in every walk of life, but I can genuinely say that all police officers I have worked with have been brilliant and wonderful human beings. I have some fantastic memories and have made some great friends.

Chapter Nineteen: The End of The Police

"If you tell the truth, you don't have to remember anything. A lie has speed but truth has endurance"

I had been thinking very hard about leaving the Police for a long time, but had not made any moves as I knew it was a step into the unknown. I never in my wildest dreams dreamt that someone else would make the decision for me and that I would be dismissed.

It was a hugely rewarding job, but it also brought with it challenges. You were often confronted with very difficult situations and you saw things that people really shouldn't have to confront. When you went home you just had to switch off from it, otherwise you would go crazy.

You can't really talk to your partner about it. They don't want to hear that you had to attend a suicide where someone hanged themselves or an accident where someone burned to death in a car. It would be unfair to share that with them. You just either bottle it up and try and make a joke of things with your colleague. There is a lot of dark humour to just try and get on can cope with what you have to deal with.

There was also the challenge of constantly moving police stations. Due to relationship changes, I seemed to move workplaces every two years and it was very reminiscent of my football career. This made it hard to settle and, being honest, I never really got back the wonderful times I had in the Manchester force. I was now working in a small town called Rotherham based in Maltby Police Station. The situation wasn't ideal and there were a number of colleagues off sick with stress, which placed more

pressure on those of us left. I was always very proud of the fact that I hadn't taken a single day off sick in my working career.

There were times when I was under intense pressure, especially around the time of the armed attack on my car, but I decided to try and control any damaging thoughts inside my head. With hindsight, I should have swallowed my pride and taken some time off or sought help, but I didn't. If you were from

Yorkshire and a cop, the expectation was that you just kept going and bottled up any negative thoughts. Instead, I used other ways to cope.

The most obvious was that I drank a lot. I have been drinking alcohol all my adult life and, as I mentioned it was often a huge part of my football career and I carried that into my personal life after I stopped playing. I never drank before games or if I knew I would be starting early at work in the Police, but after a match or after work I used alcohol to relax, sometimes drinking to crazy levels. My teammates, close friends and colleagues knew this, but I felt I have always been able to control it.

Although not an alcoholic, I would readily admit that I am dependent on alcohol to some extent. It helped me relax and forget about the pressure of football or the horrors I would have to confront as a police officer. Having irregular working hours didn't help. Footballers had a lot of time off and police work crazy shift patterns. This gave you a lot of time to indulge and alcohol was my favourite indulgence.

The other way I coped was by using the legal high of Liquid Gold. This is basically a popper or small bottle of aroma that gives a warm feeling when inhaled or sniffed. Both Jane and I used to use these on occasion, mostly around the house if we were having an evening to ourselves and wanted to relax. They are completely legal, but our text conversations about them would come back to haunt me when I was accused of taking cocaine.

My final way of coping, and the one which I believe ultimately led to my positive drugs test was stress medication I purchased off the internet from the USA. I was under a lot of pressure with work at the time, but was too proud to go to the doctors. It was stupid, but I was worried that something like that would be on my medical records forever and might be held against me or damage my career in some way. I thought I would order the medication I needed online, leaving me with a clean record. With hindsight, it was a huge error of judgement that would cost me my career, but it made complete sense to me at the time.

I had come on duty just before 7am on Saturday 19th March, 2016. It was a normal day, and we were immediately called to a domestic incident in an area called Brinsworth. My colleague, Neil Moxon and I set off with all our lights flashing and sirens blasting to respond to the call. When we arrived, we entered the mid terraced property to see a male and female arguing but no signs of any violence. They were partners and it appeared that the male had been drinking heavily.

Often in these situations, the female partner doesn't want her partner arrested but just wants him out of the house. The female stated that he has a sister next door and that he can sleep it off in there. It wasn't ideal being so close but the only other option was to arrest him and put him in the cells for a few hours.

He hadn't really done anything other than have a heated argument with his partner, so we persuaded him to come with us to his sisters and go straight to bed. We warned him that if he went back round to his partner's house then he would be arrested. We got him out and decided to park a few streets away and sit and wait for half an hour just in case he did return.

As we sat there, I received a call from my Sergeant, Darren Boulding. I assumed he was phoning to ask why we hadn't arrested the male, but instead he told me that I had to go and give a sample of breath and a drug test.

I have had random drug tests all my life in football and during my police career and for some reason they always put me on edge. I'd passed every single one and I knew I hadn't been drinking the previous night and I had never taken drugs so had no reason to be worried, but I still had that low level of stress. It was also an inconvenience to drive to the base near Sheffield. It turns out that my Sergeant has also been selected so he is there when I arrive.

I take the breath test and it is clear, so I fill out the required forms. I am then invited into another room to do the drug test. They explain everything to me and then make me turn out my pockets, presumably to make sure I don't have a sample of urine hidden on me. I am then shown the small toilet cubicle and asked to give a sample and to leave it inside the toilet for the woman to collect. After doing that, I left to carry on my shift. That night I head home not even giving the drug test a second thought.

Ten days later, my world collapses.

I am on duty and having lunch in the canteen when my Inspector, Helen Lewis walks in. She has only been with our team for several weeks and is ambitious, but a lovely person off duty. I immediately see the serious look on her face as she approaches me and immediately know something is wrong. She asks me to accompany her upstairs and we walk hardly saying a word to each other. I enter the room and there are my Sergeant and two plain clothes officers. One of the plainclothes officers, who I find out later is called Wayne Goodridge, looked straight at me and addresses the following words towards me; 'Julian Broddle, I am arresting you on suspicion of being in possession of a controlled Class A drug'.

I am stunned into numbness. I tell them that it's not true and that there must be some mistake as I have never taken drugs in my life.

Goodridge, who is from Professional Standards Department, the department of South Yorkshire Police that deals with 'bad cops' informs me that he would be taking me to another Police station to be interviewed, but that he wouldn't be putting handcuffs on me. I couldn't look at my Sergeant, Darren Boulding or Helen Lewis as I am completely embarrassed. My only thought was to get out of the office as quickly as possible so that none of my colleague see me being led away.

Once in the car, the two officers from the Professional Standards Department and I set off for Ecclesfield Police Station in Sheffield. The journey seemed to go on forever as we all tried to make awkward small talk. I am placed in a custody suite. I had brought in hundreds of prisoners in the same way throughout my career, but now here I am on the other side of the fence. The custody Sergeant wasn't happy about the fact they had arrested me on suspicion of possession of a Class A drug. He felt this was the wrong charge as the drug test occurred ten days previously. Goodridge insisted, saying that if they could find some illegal substances in my car, my police locker or in my home, then in theory I would more than likely know the substance was there and that would prove possession. Eventually, the custody sergeant was forced into accepting me, probably by someone higher up. During my eight hours in custody the Sergeant was extremely generous to me, and I regret not knowing his name to be able to thank him.

They told me that they were going to conduct searches of my property, car and locker so I was not allowed to contact anyone to prevent someone disposing of any evidence. I can only imagine how Jane felt when PSD turned up at our house and to search the entire house and garage looking for drugs.

I awaited a solicitor and after a while, also requested a Police Federation representative. He was a serving Sergeant called John Fox and was a fantastic help. It was great to have somebody there to make sure everything was ok for me. Later that evening I was interviewed by Goodridge and his colleague with my solicitor by my side.

I gave an account of where I had been a few days before the test and they wrote everything down. I was told during the interview that the quantity of illegal substances found in my system at the test had been 'off the scale'. I just couldn't believe what was happening to me. Finally, after the searches had been conducted, I was allowed to phone Jane. When I heard her voice, I could hardly talk because of the emotion.

After eight hours in custody, I was allowed to leave, but not before I had my fingerprints logged, several samples from my hair taken and my phone confiscated.

John Fox drove me back to Maltby Police Station so that I could collect my car. John did his best to be reassuring, but when I asked him to be totally upfront with me, he told me that the chances are that I will be dismissed for misconduct of a Police officer. I was in shock and things were just a blur. All I wanted to do is get home and never leave my house again.

I still have frustrations about the whole process. Most police officers I have spoken to since agreed that the arrest was unnecessary and unlawful. All the searches of my car, locker and home turned out to be negative, so there was very little evidence to base an arrest on, and eventually the arrest was deemed unlawful. They could have come to my police station having already set up John Fox and a solicitor, and interviewed me on what is called a PACE nine interview.

When I arrived home, I was exhausted. I had been working since 7am that morning and then had been in custody for eight hours. Jane was still upset from the earlier searches. Jane told me that three plainclothes officers arrived at our house, banged on the door once, then unlocked it letting themselves in and shouting that they are the Police. She was just out of the shower, so quickly got dressed to discover one male and two females at the bottom of our stairs. The male officer had been very abrupt and they went through most of the house, emptying drawers, looking through personal clothing and emptying every handbag Jane owns. At the end of the search, Jane said the male officer tried to make a joke of it, but by this point she was very distressed and in no mood to laugh.

I was advised to take leave for the next couple of days to be able to process what has happened. I was amazed at all the messages I received in those two days from colleagues once they had found out what had happened. Every message was one of support and they gave me the encouragement to contact a few colleagues, which was an enormous help at the time.

A few days later I had to go to Rotherham Main Street Station, which I was dreading as I knew my shift was on duty. I hoped to get in and out unnoticed but when the lift door opened, there was one of my closest colleagues, Steve Brass. He looked at me and gave me a pat on the back and offered a few lovely words of support. It was an emotional moment. I signed some forms, not really knowing what they were, as my head was in a spin. I just wanted to get out.

Most Police officers in my situation would automatically go off sick with stress. I decided that I had done nothing wrong and that it was a misunderstanding that would eventually be cleared up, so I wanted to carry on working and keep my never having a sick day record going. It was agreed that I would work in the staff office doing work for the senior officers.

I worked with Al Beaver and Phil Connell who were great guys and kept me going with some laughs when I needed it most. Phil in particular, became a great friend and would go on to give me the greatest support I could ever wish for.

Not long after my arrest, I went to see my Inspector, Helen Lewis, and asked her if I could attend my

Police Station when my team were coming on duty to explain what had happened. I had nothing to hide and felt it was only right to face my colleagues. Helen agreed and a couple of days later, I headed to Maltby Police Station. Talking to my team was one of the hardest things I've ever done but it was wonderful to get their support and it made me feel better just letting it out.

Eventually, John Fox got in touch saying that PSD were ready for another interview as the information from my phone and my hair sample had come back from being analysed. Before the interview my solicitor met with the team to go over the new evidence. It was not good news. My solicitor said that the hair samples showed I was a regular user of cocaine and that they had lots of text conversations between Jane and I that made it look like I was 'bang at it' doing drugs. He advised me to go no comment throughout the entire interview process. I couldn't quite believe it, but I took his advice.

The interview was frustrating as hell. They were presenting text messages between us referring to 'sniffy stuff' and assumed we were talking about cocaine. I could have told them this in seconds that was what we called the Liquid Gold we occasionally took, which was perfectly legal, but it didn't matter. Every response had to be 'no comment'. After it was over and I was alone with John Fox and my solicitor they told me that there was too much damaging evidence and that I would be more than likely dismissed when the evidence is presented at a hearing.

The room was silent and there was very little else that could be said. It was a devastating moment. I immediately called my welfare office and told her that I was going off sick, for the first time in my police career. I knew it was over and that I was finished. I got home and explained the situation to Jane. There was nothing we could do. I couldn't explain why my hair sample had shown that I was a regular user of cocaine. At that moment, I was numb and lost.

For the next few days, I couldn't think straight. I even blamed Jane for my predicament, convincing myself that she must have stupidly got hold of this stuff from somewhere and be adding it to my drink on nights out. It was stupid and I deeply regret thinking that, but I was all over the place and not thinking logically. Eventually, the fog lifted and I realised that it was most probably the medication I had bought on the internet and been using off and on to help me cope with stress.

I had no idea what was in it and I can only assume that there were traces of cocaine somewhere in the mix. I had none left and had bought it so long ago that I didn't even have a record of what website I'd found it on. I knew there was no way that I could prove that to clear my name and it was clear from the interview process that they had already made up their minds that I was guilty. I knew I had to just brace myself for the hearing and prepare for a future without the Police.

I had told my workmates about what happened, but telling my family, my brothers and my children wasn't so easy. I couldn't face them so left it until I was finally leaving the Police. I can't thank people enough for my friends and colleagues who supported me during that difficult time. I was asked out a few times by my work colleagues and we would catch a train to Sheffield and go for a drink.

My workmates would just take the piss, asking me where they could get a hit and asking me to help them. I was used to the abuse from my football days and laughing about it made it a little easier to cope with the harsh reality of the situation.

My final hearing was scheduled for December 20th 2016, an early Christmas present from South Yorkshire Police. John Fox and I talked at length and agreed that I now had no option but to accept guilt and that I should not attend the hearing. John would attend and represent me. He would give a speech on my behalf, apologising for the position I had put myself in and then mention my commendations and previous police record. I had hoped that this would be the end of it. How wrong could I be?

A few days before the hearing the Sheffield, Rotherham and Barnsley Star heard about the case and ran a story on it. A policeman being sacked was of interest in itself, but when that policeman played for Sheffield United and Barnsley then it was too good an opportunity to resist. It soon went national across the UK.

I was hounded by reporters and abused on social media as people found out the details of the case. There was nothing I could do but keep my head down and take it. I knew I would have to live with the consequences of being branded a 'dodgy cop'.

I was in Hull when John phoned to tell me that the hearing was over and that I was no longer a Police officer.

So where am I now. Having been dismissed by South Yorkshire Police, I decided that I wouldn't let it beat me and I wanted to move on as quickly as possible onto the next chapter. I decided to start looking for jobs. This was harder than I realised. At first, I thought I could use my experience as a long serving Police officer in a similar role, so started going for every law enforcement officer jobs and the like.

I knew my CV would be ok regarding my life experiences and that I had a long list of professional football clubs on it, that I was reasonably confident somebody would take a look at the CV and think that I had a very colourful history of employment and would at the very least, give me an interview. I sat in my house completing application form after application form and then waited for the phone calls.

I thought I would get quite a few and I felt confident about my interviewing skills. Afterall, how hard can it be talking about yourself. I had been a guest at some of my previous football clubs and had to stand up and talk about my times in the game in front of strangers, and that wasn't a problem, so doing interviews would be no problem. I think in the first few weeks, I must have done fifty applications and probably got back three interviews. The interviews I got were for part time security and law enforcement. I had to do something, until another opportunity came around so off I went to the interviews.

As expected, the interviews went well. I felt reasonably confident and waited for the companies to get back to me. In the end, two of these people called me and gave me the truth. They both said that my interviews were fantastic. However, once they had done their references checks with my previous employer, it resulted in that South Yorkshire Police were informing them that I had been dismissed. When they then googled me, it showed all the negative media and press about that I was sacked for taking cocaine.

Under the circumstances, these people calling me just couldn't take a chance. I really appreciated their honesty as I was not aware what was on the references from the Police. It was clear that I had no chance of getting any job as the cocaine issue would keep coming back to haunt me. Basically, something that could now be explained, will follow me forever, and I could apply for fifty jobs, and maybe, one company just might give me a chance, and that's if the people making the decision were football fans of a club I played for and would give me a chance.

I wasn't prepared to keep applying for like-minded jobs and keep getting knocked back and deflated. I did have things in the pipeline, and my brilliant mate, Phil Connell, was asking everybody he knew to try and get me a job. I knew that I would have to do something self-employed, until I got help. I have worked all my life from leaving school in 1981. I have played professional football all over England and Scotland, and never once have I felt so useless as I do now.

I took drug tests all the time in football and never ever thought about it being a positive result, and felt the same way when taking drug tests in the Police. I am told that I am the very first Police officer in South Yorkshire Police to be dismissed for having failed a drug test for cocaine. I am not sure if the Police would accept what I have since found out about why the test was positive, but I suppose I can put it in my book, and hope the real people that know me, know I would never do such a stupid action and treat me the way they use to.

Chapter Twenty:
Reflections

"The first to apologise is the bravest, the first to forgive is the strongest, and the first to forget is the happiest"

So where am I now? It has been almost six months since I was dismissed by South Yorkshire Police. I have now had time to reflect on the difficult events that led to the end of my police career. I slowly have come to terms with the fact that the police is now a part of my past and I am now looking to the future. All I can do is move on and take that terrible experience in my life and try and turn it into a positive. I now have the chance to experience other opportunities in life, rather than being tied to the police service.

If there has been one encouraging aspect of the last year, it has been the support and kindness from friends. The messages of support I have received from school friends, family, colleagues and former teammates have been overwhelming. They say that only when you are at your lowest do you find out who your true friends are. I have been very lucky to discover that I am a rich man when it comes to the friendships I have made throughout my football and police career.

I have also been humbled by the fact that supporters of many of the clubs I have played for have taken time out to contact me on social media and offer their support. It is something I appreciate greatly. I am also extremely fortunate to have such a loving partner as Jane. We have slowly worked through the stresses and pain my dismissal has caused us and we had to be very strong together to get through it. We have used each other as our rock when it has got too much and we are a stronger couple for it.

I know that the legacy of my dismissal will never truly go away. The media interest may have died down but much of the damage to my reputation has been done and technology nowadays means that an online search for Julian Broddle will likely always produce the lurid headlines. I know there will be many others, perhaps even those who have made it this far in this book, that will doubt my story and believe that there is no smoke without fire. I know I cannot convince the doubters, but I am happy that the people close to me accept the truth.

Writing this book has been very therapeutic way of coping with the wrongful arrest and my subsequent dismissal. I originally started writing just to have a memoir to pass on to my grown-up children, but being able to put down on paper my story has helped me reflect on the career in football that I did have and come to terms with recent events.

Sitting here, reflecting on life, I realised that I have a few regrets. I sometimes regret not thinking before I jumped in to the next part of my life. I should have sometimes just sat back and considered my options more and then I just might not have made some of the mistakes that I did. That is true of every aspect of my life including my football career, my time in the police and in my relationships. I do wonder whether I should have stayed longer at the places I lived. I seemed to move around the country every two years on average. What if I had stayed and fought for my place in that particular team, or stayed at Greater Manchester Police where I loved working?

My biggest personal regret is that, after my divorce, I never really worked hard enough to keep close to my children. Thanks to their mother, they have grown up to be wonderful individuals with great character and strong ethics and morals. I hope that I played a small part in helping them grow in the short time I was in there in their lives as children. Regardless of whether I did or not, I am immensely proud of the adults they have become.

Writing this book has made me look back on the career I had and reflect on what I did accomplish. As a footballer, you are sometimes caught up in the moment and don't take in what you or your teammates achieved.

I look back on it now and I am incredibly proud. I had a great career at some wonderful clubs and achieved a lot, especially latterly at Raith Rovers. I played a lot of games and have some incredible memories and I know a lot of people would have given their right arm for a career like mine. With hindsight, I perhaps should have thought about trying to get some other job in football after I stopped playing, but at the time I just wanted out and to experience the real world.

My only slight regret is that I think I should have believed in myself more as a footballer and looked after myself better. I think if my head had have been different, if my diet had have been a bit better, I could have played at a higher level and achieved the one big move that I was looking for. I was a drinker, the food I ate was terrible and I never drank enough fluids. If I'd really focused on my nutrition and if I had the right mental attitude with no self-doubt, then I am convinced I could have had a shot at a higher level.

I appreciate the privileged life I had as a young man, but I wish I could have only able to bottle up those moments when I ran onto the football pitch full of confidence and knowing that I would have a great game. But then who knows where I would have ended up or what I would have achieved.

If I had gone to a top club, then I may have not ended up at Raith Rovers and I would never have experienced the joy of beating Celtic to win the League Cup, securing promotion to the Premier League and facing the giants of Bayern Munich in European competition.

I may never have sat in the Olympic Stadium at half-time, with the gaffer laughing at the fact that were leading 1-0 and the Bayern manager losing the plot in the dressing room next door. These are great memories that I would not trade for the world.

This book has also made me realise that the greatest joy of my football and police career have been the people have met and the friends I have made. To have worked in two careers where I had the chance to be part of a team and to develop friendships that last a lifetime has been an absolute privilege. I would like to say a huge thank you to all my friends and colleague at Hazel Grove, Stockport, Bolton, Farnworth, Ashton Under Lyne, Maltby and Rotherham police stations. We had some brilliant times at work and when off duty. I would like to say the same thank you to all my teammates over the years at the football clubs I played at.

The lads at Sheffield United, Scunthorpe, Barnsley, Plymouth Argyle, St Mirren, Partick Thistle, Raith Rovers, East Fife and Ross County. We had some great times on and off the field. To have been lucky enough to have made a career out of playing football was an absolute honour and I still miss it.

I miss the team spirit and the banter.

I miss being fit.

I miss working two hours a day.

I miss the nights out and trips we had.

I miss the appreciation from fans when you did well.

But sitting here, years down the line, the memories still make me smile and I am thankful for every last minute. It was truly a privilege.

Playing Career Statistics

Years	Team	Apps	(Gls)
1981–1983	Sheffield United	1	(0)
1983–1987	Scunthorpe United	134	(32)
1987–1990	Barnsley	77	(4)
1990	Plymouth Argyle	9	(0)
1990–1992	St Mirren	59	(2)
1992–1993	→ Scunthorpe United (loan)	6	(0)
1992	Partick Thistle	5	(0)
1993–1996	Raith Rovers	73	(1)

1996	East Fife	6	(0)
1996–1997	Ross County	29	(0)
Total		**399**	**(39)**

One More Thing Before You Go…

f you enjoyed reading this book or found it useful, I'd be very grateful if you'd post a short review on Amazon.

Your support really does make a difference, and I read all the reviews personally, so I can get your feedback and make this book even better.

If you'd like to leave a review, then all you need to do is click the review link on Amazon here:

And if you live in the UK, you can leave it here:

If you would like to contact me: mailto:jbted11@gmail.com

Thanks again for your support!

Printed in Great Britain
by Amazon

23387585R00162